"Shocking, pit-in-your stomach moments reveal a raw and very real narrative of how growing up experiences can hold us back in adulthood. This would be an important read for teens entering a precarious time in life. Equally important, it's a read for parents to change family patterning and make better choices. Carol gives comprehensive tools in the book that provide how-to exercises to become more self-aware and to start living from a place of perseverance and purpose."

—Randy Spelling, Freedom Strategist and Business Coach, Author of *Unlimiting You: Step Out of Your Past and Into Your Purpose*

"If you are looking for inspiration and the right blend of courage and grit, take hold of Carol Lopez's book, *Muck Off!* Carol's raw and revealing story of what it takes to tackle a challenging and, at best, defeating past and use that emotion to catapult herself into an intentionally designed life of grace and new beginnings is beautiful. Her empathy and love for those she shares her story with shines through in her writing, and the breakthroughs she has made as a natural leader and coach will inspire you to take the wheel of your own life and make the changes you desire."

—Theresa Callahan, Author of *Managing for Performance: Building Accountability for Team Success*

"Carol has written a heartfelt, honest and healing book that will assist others in going from Victim to Victor, from Fear to Faith. Read this book and give it to a loved one who is "Stuck in the Muck!" They will thank you!"

—Mark Matteson, Best Selling Author of *Freedom from Fear*

"Carol Lopez has written a sometimes surprising, straightforward, honest, and self-revealing book with the sole purpose of helping us avoid disaster, own our problems, and actually live our lives. Readers will find themselves engaged in her own personal story while learning a holistic approach to taking control of their own lives and living the best possible version of themselves that they can. She manages to package up all of this advice with plain language, real insights, practical steps, and a humility that desires to put God first and make living worshipful. If you have struggled with life or want to avoid creating unnecessary struggle, pick up this book, settle down for an evening, and get ready to laugh, empathize, and *learn something new that will help you tomorrow.*"

—Christian Lindbeck, Lead Pastor, Hillcrest Chapel, Bellingham, Washington

"Carol Lopez has been through the muck and lived to tell the tale. The thing is she's fully aware that going through the muck comes with a responsibility—to shake it off and then teach others how to do the same. In this powerful book, she reveals how to overcome dysfunctional behaviors, how to develop a spiritual relationship with God, and how to pursue your dreams. A better life awaits, and it can begin for you in these pages."

—Tyler R. Tichelaar, PhD and award-winning author of *Narrow Lives* and *The Best Place*

"Typically, when you are in the 'muck' in your own life, you tend to think you are all by yourself. No one could possibly be dealing with the same kinds of horrible situations. Carol's courage to share her story in this book will have you feeling connected to the author and realizing you're not alone. And because you're not alone, you can apply the same strategies Carol shares to get out of your own muck. This book will help you create the life you deserve in a shorter amount of time."

—Kieran Murry, Author of *Go for Your Gold*

"Carol Lopez takes a reflecting journey to get the muck off her life! *Muck Off* is an account of the author's life from where she has been to where she wants to be, from the life she has had to the life she wants to live. Very beneficial to anyone interested in self-reflection."

—Seconde Nimenya, MBA, International Award-Winning Author of *Evolving Through Adversity* and *A Hand to Hold*

"Carol Lopez's story of hope and healing will draw you in to her process of how to get rid of the 'muck' in your life. She opens up about the reality of her life challenges and demonstrates for us how she is victorious over those difficulties. *Muck Off* is a great book to have in your library!"

—Sue Mocker, Author of *The Hope Factor* and Chief Ambassador of Hope Allowed

"You don't have to settle for a life of disappointment and disgust. Instead, you can discover the destiny that awaits you. Carol Lopez has found it, and in *Muck Off*, she reveals how, no matter how far down in the muck you are, you can rise above your situation to have a fulfilling, purposeful, and enjoyable life."

—Patrick Snow, Publishing Coach and International Best-Selling Author of *Creating Your Own Destiny* and *Boy Entrepreneur*

MUCK OFF

THE STARTING POINT TO YOUR HAPPILY EVER AFTER

CAROL L. LOPEZ

Muck Off: The Starting Point to Your Happily Ever After

www.MuckOffBook.com

Published by:
Author Academy Elite
P.O. Box 43
Powell, OH 43065

Paperback: 978-1-640-85-278-5
Hardback: 978-1-64085-279-2
Ebook: 978-1-64085-280-8

Editor: Tyler Tichelaar
Cover Photo: Shelly Forsberg, Forsberg Photography
Cover Design: Shiloh Schroeder, Fusion Works
Interior Book Design: JetLaunch.net
Sketches: Uzuri Designs

Every attempt has been made to properly source all quotes.

Printed in the United States of America

First Edition

Disclaimer: Many, but not all, of the names, locations, and actual events have been changed to protect the privacy of those involved.

In Loving Memory of My Mom and Dad,
Charlotte L. Craddock and Charles J. Craddock

Glory to God

ACKNOWLEDGMENTS

Not only does it take a village to raise a child; apparently, it takes one to birth a book. Special thanks to special people: Thank you, my one and only brother, Michael Craddock, who told me I should write a book and for believing in me to get it done. I love you unconditionally and cherish our relationship. Thank you, Marco Lopez, my loving husband, for being a catalyst for some of my healing and for taking care of the household duties during the times I quarantined myself to write. To my niece, Chantal Maupin, who took the time to read the first draft and provided feedback with encouragement to continue. To my sons, I love you unconditionally and always will. All of you helped me grow, heal, and become a better person.

I acknowledge those in my life who have at one point or another assisted with my personal growth: Marco Lopez, Michael Craddock, Helen Hunt, Mark Matteson, Randy Spelling, Kat Kim, Theresa Callahan, and so many others. Thank you, friends, for providing your support and valuable feedback: Jason Hale, Karen Steward, Laura McLeod, and Melissa Velasquez.

My technical support people who helped me start from ground zero to published author: Patrick Snow, Tyler Tichelaar, Shiloh Schroeder, and Kary Oberbrunner.

Thank you to everyone who encouraged me and prayed for me. Your support and friendship mean more to me than words can describe. I'm truly grateful for your love.

CONTENTS

INTRODUCTION
KNOWING THE WHY BEHIND THE WHAT

Muck! Muck! MUUUUCKK! You know what it is! It's all the crap that tears you apart, breaks your heart, and spits you out leaving you feeling empty, exhausted, burnt, and bewildered. You've tried to remain intact but somewhere along the way you've lost—you. Only your fragile shell remains. You no longer have the bold courage and confidence you once had. Those things have been stripped away and replaced with anger, resentment, shame, and guilt. Not only have you lost you, but also your dreams. Again, you are left standing in line to ride on the merry-go-round of insanity. You repeat self-defeating behaviors only hoping for a new result. You are not alone. . . . I've been there before.

I was born a perfect princess. I had the blessings of being the baby of the family and the only redhead. From the outside, people who don't know me think I have lived the perfect life. Ha! My life has been far from perfect. I'm going to share with you my most traumatic experiences and idiotic, stupid mistakes. Why? Because if I can spare you pain, I will. If the pain already exists, then let's turn your pain into your passion.

This princess has woken the muck up and is no longer a sleeping beauty. No longer will I be a doormat for life to just happen. I have no tolerance for the power and control others have used to try to entrap me. I am free to be me. I am able to dream again and live from my essence. I am beautiful, unstoppable light; joyful and real, living in aesthetic creative flight! It took me years of healing, searching, and internal work to really know myself again. Many times, I've lived on a wing and a prayer, meaning I wasn't fully prepared; however, I had faith that success would come. Hoping wasn't enough and I needed to work on myself. Through this work, I found forgiveness, unconditional love, and faith. My prayers got me through the craziest times. I've been through the muck, and I can be of assistance to you. Let me help you prepare for your best life ever! I would love to be your co-pilot in creating your happily ever after.

If you could live a life of no regrets, would you do it? Hell yeah, you would! You would because no one likes pain. I've experienced enough pain to last me a lifetime, and I realized a lot of the pain could have been prevented. A broken heart is one of the hardest things to heal, but a broken heart does not need to define you or your life. You may be so broken you don't want to live anymore. Or you may be hopelessly entrenched in the muck and you can't see or think clearly. Or perhaps you try to dismiss and ignore it all, shrug it off, and say, "Meh, shit happens!" Yes, "life happens," and "muck happens." However, I'm here to tell you it wasn't meant to be this way! You can prevent the muck from happening in your life. Prevent it, use it, chew it up, and spit it out as your purpose!

Are you ready to get off the merry-go-round of insanity? Are you absolutely frustrated with where you are in your life? If yes, great! This is exactly where you need to be—at a place of willingness; willing to do whatever it takes to change! Being in a place of willingness means you are open to accept simple suggestions, which is exactly what this book is offering—a suggestion to catapult you into a life you thought was not possible!

The ownership of your journey lies in your hands. Once you understand the true power behind this and make the decision to start living for you, it will begin to happen! It will be as if people magically appear in support of your dreams and doors will open. You will have no choice but to stop mucking around! It all starts with the decision. Your talents were meant to be a gift to the world. It's time to share them. My biggest wish for you is to live your happily ever after. Don't let your "Once upon a time," slip by you. The time to make this happen is now!

Are you ready to explode with enthusiasm for life again? Are you ready to live the rest of your life doing those things you absolutely love? Are you ready to smile every day because you know you made a difference? If yes, then stop mucking around with this introduction and turn the page!

Cheers to a new life!

With gratitude and love,

Carol Lopez

SECTION ONE

REFLECT

I WAS BORN A PERFECT PRINCESS AND THEN . . .
MUCK HAPPENED.

When this princess looked in the mirror, she saw an image that was not of herself, yet there were glimmers of what was once there. Upon further reflection on the environment from which she originated, the decisions she made, the consequences of those decisions, and her response to all of these, she better understood herself. She gained clarity and hope for a better tomorrow.

Section One of this book focuses on reflection. What's important about reflecting? Getting clear on the lessons you've learned in an effort not to repeat them! Taking a look back at your past may be scary. However, reflecting will give you strength. After all, look at what you've already gotten past and accomplished! This is the beginning of a journey to feeling better and doing the things you love. Reflecting reveals where things went wrong and provides insight into areas of personal growth, which is essential to becoming your best self and living your best life.

1

REBELLING AGAINST ABANDONMENT

"Rebellion is a sign of a child fighting to be seen as who they are."

—Carol Tuttle

Not knowing what to expect and with a knot in my stomach, I dreadfully open the front door to my parents' house. As soon as I enter, a punch lands on my cheek! The claw of my mom's fingernails penetrates my arm as she jerks me toward her. I fly into the Christmas tree, sparks flash, and I hear ornaments shatter around me as I fall to the floor. My eyes tightly close with anticipation of the next blow. The blow didn't come. I open my eyes and there's my dad with a gun pointed at me. I am the target! My brother tries to get the gun from my dad. I'm stuck between them. I lean forward to avoid the gun being held to my temple. I freeze. My brother wrestles my dad to the ground and I watch him peel my dad's fingers, one-by-one, off the gun.

My brother quickly pushes the gun under the couch. I am saved! The fight is over.

There is a moment of silence wherein each one of us gathers our shock and disbelief. We come back to sanity. All of us are freaked out in our own way. The four of us—my dad, mom, brother, and I—form a circle, linking arms. I vow to stop seeing my boyfriend.

A surreal moment. As I head upstairs, I stop and slowly turn around. My mom and brother silently stand in the living room still gathering themselves. I thought to myself, "They *are* crazy!" My dad is on all fours looking under the couch for the gun that moments before he held to my head *and* pulled the trigger! As I paused in this moment, it registered, "He *really* did try to *kill* me!" This is real!

Imagining my dad killing me is unfathomable. *The* dad who took his little princess out for ice cream, carnivals, and Disney movies, making an attempt, and a damned good one to end my life doesn't make sense.

The day my dad put a gun to my head has been forever labeled as "the gun incident." As much as I would like to forget this day ever happened, it impacted me in ways I never realized until I started to write about it. It all started when I heard my dad say, "I brought her into this world, and I will take her out of this world." I crept toward the stairwell and listened closely. Then I ran to the bedroom and repeated what I heard to my sister. My dad was filled with anger, and his voice naturally carried upstairs. As the plan continued to unfold, he said, "I will take off all her clothes and throw her out in the snow!" I felt anxious and didn't know what to do.

Normally, people don't literally mean such phrases when they say them. I wondered now, *Did they not know I was upstairs? Did they not think I could hear them?* My gut told me he meant what he said and my instinct was to flee. I told my sister I wasn't going to wait around for it to happen. I was out of there.

To escape, I went across the hall to the big room. It was separated from the rest of the upstairs. Outside the rear-facing window was a roof to a screened-in patio, except it was no longer screened in due to wear and tear over the years. I stepped out onto the roof and jumped. I ran to my boyfriend's house.

When I got to my boyfriend's house, I told his mom everything my parents were saying. She told me I needed to call my parents to let them know where I was and then go back home. I knew she thought she was doing the right thing by telling me I had to go back. Reluctantly, I called home. In a commanding voice, my mom said, "Stay there; I'm coming to get you with a shotgun!" I hung up and stayed put like she told me.

So much for my big escape! I'm not sure what I was thinking when I went to my boyfriend's house. Maybe it wasn't the best place to go because my boyfriend was the enemy in my parents' eyes since they defined him solely by his being black. His family was like family to me, so perhaps I was thinking they would take me in as one of their own. Now I had no place to go. No one knew at this time what was really in store for me.

I was relieved to see it was my brother picking me up. I wasn't old enough to drive, so someone had to come get me. I don't recall what the conversation was in the car on the way home, but I remember his teasing comment, "You did it now." My brother, being a big brother, rubbed it in that I was the one in trouble, not him. For me, it was a very solemn moment. I was scared. I had never been in this kind of trouble before and I didn't know what to expect. My dad was the kind of dad who could look at you and make you cower. Up until the "gun incident" my dad had never laid a finger on me.

My brother saved my life. No words can express the love and gratitude I have for my courageous brother. Something changed in me that day. I realized I was no longer safe in my home. My own parents could not be trusted not to harm me. The only one I could rely on was myself, and I needed to find a way out.

I had nowhere to turn. I would sit in my room and pray to God to get me out of there. I even wrote my prayer, "God, get me out of here," in pencil on the frame of my closet door—so small that no one ever saw it. All of this led to my first experience with depression. I would sleep a lot to escape.

The idea of going to college didn't seem to fit me. There were never any discussions in my house about what I would do upon graduation or what college I would attend. There was no expectation for me to do anything other than "Turn out right because you are the last one!" Looking back, I wondered why no one called the police during the gun incident. After the incident, life went on as if the incident had never happened. Nothing was resolved; only on the surface. I continued to see my boyfriend.

During the early 1980s, the neighborhood was segregated. I grew up in a suburb on the South Side of Chicago. The whites lived on one side of the highway and the blacks lived on the other. My boyfriend lived on the black side, in an area known as Canterbury.

I reflected on the statement my brother made to me, "You should have been dead." Under the circumstances, had the gun not jammed, there is a high probability I would not be here. Apparently, I wasn't meant to be dead. A relevant scripture that resonates with me is:

"For I know the plans I have for you," declares the Lord,
"plans to prosper you and not harm you, plans to give you
hope and a future."
—Jeremiah 29:11

This verse reflects one of God's promises for you. It gave me hope and confirmation for not only being alive but also to live out my purpose.

Perhaps you've lived through something and it resonates with you too. If it works for you, consider making this verse your daily affirmation. Say it to yourself every day; let it confirm for you that your life has a purpose. You were not meant to be dead! You are valuable. You made it here, and there is a reason why you made it. God doesn't make mistakes!

BEING PREJUDICE

> *"Racism is taught in our society, it is not automatic.*
> *It is learned behavior toward persons with dissimilar*
> *physical characteristics."*
> —Alex Haley

The gap between my parents' point of view and mine on interracial relationships widened. I learned how people with prejudicial views act, although I could not understand it. My boyfriend was half-white, so in my mind, he wasn't black. He was half-white and half-black. I quickly learned society viewed any person with any amount of African-American blood as black.

Anglo-Saxon people have historically had privilege in American society. To preserve this privilege, it was viewed as important to keep the blood unmixed. I never felt privileged. I worked hard for everything I've ever acquired and accomplished. When we understand where stigmas come from, we can deal with them from an educated perspective. I often wonder how my life might have turned out differently if my father had not rejected me. Had my father accepted my boyfriend, I wonder whether it would have affected my other choices later in life. If my dad showed me unconditional love without judgment, what choices would I have made?

I've been around the block when it comes to this topic of prejudice. I've been rejected by people of all races for various reasons. When it comes to black folks, the rejection I have received is only a smidgeon of the pain they have encountered in comparison. There have been other times I've also been more accepted by them than my own race. Being on the receiving end of prejudice feels like the ultimate form of rejection.

Have you felt prejudice, either directly or through observation? Parents' comments often have an impact on how children view the world. My parents were broken-hearted over the fact that I was growing up and choosing to be with someone they did not approve of due to their own prejudices.

It wasn't until years later, when I reflected back on this story, that I realized I had been rebelling against my parents. This was a great epiphany for me because I didn't even realize it was rebellion, nor did I know the root cause of it. I was a child fighting to be seen for who I was, and instead, I was abandoned and then later rejected for my choices.

ABANDONMENT

And why didn't I listen to my parents? A psychologist once told me I was abandoned as a child. While I hadn't thought of myself as abandoned, the day I left the counselor's office, I was left without knowing how to process this idea of abandonment. I was not neglected physically. I had lived in the same house for eighteen years of my life, and I had always had nice clothes and good food to eat. My basic physical needs were met.

Emotionally, however, I likened it to being raised like a cat. I was merely there, in existence to pet and play with when it was convenient for those in the house and to bring comfort to others. I was given adult responsibilities while my mom worked nights. My dad was not emotionally present for me and rarely was he physically present because he was often passed out on the couch.

Recently, I took a deep dive into the vault where the abandonment laid dormant for years and unraveled what it meant to me. The abandonment penetrated my subconscious and left a scar on me of not feeling valued by my parents. I was oblivious to the fact that I had low self-esteem and did not know how to value myself. It's no wonder the rest of my life played out the way it did. Of course, if my parents were alive today, they would say they loved me very much. But this story is not about them, but rather, how I process my life and respond to it. And sharing what I have learned will hopefully provide you with a deeper understanding of your life.

Yes, perhaps I had been abandoned. But once I had a label for my experience, I used it to work my way through those feelings. I refused to go through life making excuses for myself because I had been "abandoned." We all have a choice whether to live by these labels or not. Live your life by who you are, and not by what someone else puts on you.

LESSONS LEARNED

Holding a gun to my head wasn't enough to keep me away from the boy I loved. I was subconsciously rebelling against abandonment. Had the relationship with my parents been different from an early age, I might have respected them enough to listen. Since the third grade, they had not been physically or emotionally present for me.

After I left home, I recall stopping dead in my tracks one day and thinking to myself, *I have no one to answer to. I am grown and I am my own person. I'm not living in the pressure can anymore. I do not have to think, talk, act, or believe in the same things as my parents.* I felt free. I believe my parents tried to give their kids a better life than they had, although I don't know much about their lives.

In my quest for understanding myself better, I realize this is an area where I was on autopilot. I was an adolescent living in an adult world. I was not living my life according to my values because the discussion of concrete values was not directly communicated. And it goes deeper than this because low self-esteem and the avoidance of abandonment through rebellion resulted in promiscuity. Freud called this a form of *"repetition compulsion*: An unconscious adult re-enactment of seeking love from but being rejected, uncared for and abandoned by her emotionally and physically unavailable parents."

I have become a self-supporting, self-sufficient, independent woman from all of this so-called "abandonment." I am not a victim. I cannot go back and change my childhood. My parents are both deceased now, and I know they did their best with what they were taught. During my mom's last few months of life, she shared with me how she felt so guilty for working outside the home. I now wish I had this insight sooner so I could talk about this in greater depth with her and tell her I'm sorry for breaking her heart.

Sadly, I am afraid I have repeated this cycle in raising my own children. I hope my children forgive me for the things they have yet to discover about the effects of their upbringing.

Labels help us process information, but they do not have to rule our lives. The best gift I learned is to know I have value and purpose to serve in this world. I choose to live in a positive light. Every life is valuable. Please recognize your value!

SUMMARY

When I fell in love with a biracial young man, I was unaware of what being prejudice meant, let alone how my parents felt and the impact of these views. The Civil Rights Act of 1964 had passed years before I was even in diapers. There isn't any one person who is better than the other. We all are called to something greater than ourselves. Fighting for power and control creates tension, and no one wins in the end. Think about how you are responding to specific situations. What would happen if you and I were known for our ability to love?

My childhood wasn't the worst, and it wasn't the best. I've learned that if you tell your children they are good, you will get good children. I was a good child—good at performing my chores and keeping the peace. I was good in my parents' eyes until I dated someone they disapproved of. If you call your daughter a slut, what do you think you will get? Think about what would happen if, instead, you told your child she was creative, resourceful, capable, and intelligent. Stay away from negative labels and use appropriate ones to process through the situation. Learning to discredit negative labels that were put upon you as a child takes awareness and practice.

There is power in the tongue. Proverbs 18:21 states, "The tongue has the power of life and death, and those who love it will eat its fruit." I cannot stress enough how important this is in raising your kids. Your kids will make mistakes, and how you respond with your words will be life-altering—for better or worse.

I held on to the feedback given to me by a psychologist. I wish I had taken the time when I received the feedback to understand fully the meaning behind it. Had I done this personal work long ago, I'm sure my children would have made different choices in their lives because I would have been present more physically and emotionally. You do not need to let the muck define you or your life, and I believe you can prevent passing down the muck to the next generation. By reflecting and getting to know yourself better, you become a better you and a better parent.

REFLECTION QUESTIONS

When have you felt rejected or abandoned?

_____

_____

_____

_____

_____

_____

What messages did you hear growing up?

_____

_____

_____

_____

_____

_____

How did these messages play out in your life?

_____

_____

_____

_____

_____

_____

_____

_____

_____

_____

_____

_____

_____

What will you choose to do with the labels, messages, and things said to you?

_____

_____

_____

_____

_____

What positive messages do you want your children to hear growing up?

_____

_____

_____

_____

_____

How will you show your children they are valued?

_____

_____

_____

_____

_____

How will you be present, both emotionally and physically, for your children?

_____

_____

_____

_____

_____

2

MAKING A LIFE-IMPACTING DECISION

"Life is really simple, but we insist on making it complicated."

—Confucius

In Chapter 1, you learned no matter how you are treated or what you experience, you are called to something greater than your circumstances. When you value yourself, your decisions in life will also reflect this value. No matter what labels are put on you, you get to choose whether you accept them or not. There is power in the tongue, so use it to speak positive affirmations. In this chapter, you will see how my rebellious behaviors continued and brought about consequences—life-changing consequences.

HORRIFIC EXPERIENCE

Swoosh! I made it. I graduated high school. I was soon to be nineteen years old, and I figured out my grand escape from my home was to join the United States Navy! Nothing was going to stop me. My plan was to use the Navy as a way to get to California so I could fulfill my big dream of becoming a model. I thought if I could be a model, I could use this platform to become a role model for other girls. If I made it to California, I would be "discovered." The plan ended there. I didn't have the "how" figured out. Balancing a Navy career and a modeling career and what each of these really entailed—clueless. Duty stations weren't guaranteed. Leaving home, perhaps a bit brainwashed by the television theme song from *The Beverly Hillbillies,* I knew, "California is the place you ought to be."

There was at least some planning and preparation for Navy life. My junior year in high school, I entered the delayed entry program and worked hard to prepare for boot camp. I made it through all of the screening processes and then took the Oath. I was excited to go to Florida for boot camp and I was ready! Not so fast—I'm pregnant now! Life came to a complete halt. I didn't know what to do. I was pregnant by the *same* boyfriend my dad almost killed me over. *What am I going to do now?*

I confided in my sister and she told my mom! Again, no support whatsoever to keep my baby. In desperation, my boyfriend and I turned to his mom. I remember her telling us we couldn't make it. I went out and looked for an apartment. My situation started to look bleak. I felt pressure from both his family and my own to get an abortion. My boyfriend, now the father of my child, even gave in! I told him I wasn't going to pay for it. This was a turning point for me in our relationship. I thought, *How does he love me if he is willing to kill our baby?* I felt hopeless and alone. I had no answers. I wanted my baby. There was no one to turn to and no known resources. This was well before the internet explosion where you could find an answer for almost anything if you "Googled" it. I don't even know whether shelters existed at this time. If they did, I sure didn't know about them.

There was one more person I needed to tell—my recruiter. He informed me joining the military while pregnant was not an option. The military also would not allow single parents to join. This was another point of pressure. Everywhere I turned, I felt defeated. I was outnumbered. There was no place to go.

The decision to have an abortion was made based on being in a state of hopelessness. I got on my knees and prayed to God to forgive me. I said, "Forgive me, Father, for I know not what I am about to do." Meaning, the totality of the situation was incomprehensible. "God, please forgive me for what I am about to do!" I was absolutely devastated. Even with these hopeless circumstances, how could I kill my own baby?

One of my sisters knew exactly where to take me. I went to the abortion clinic and had a small white stick, which looked like one of those plant food spikes, inserted in me. A plant food spike is inserted below the soil and releases food to the roots. The spike that was inserted in me created labor pains that would lead to the abortion. I was given strict orders not to take it out or it would cause a lot of problems and make the situation worse. I wanted to rip it out of me, but the people at the clinic scared me enough with the consequences that I followed their orders.

I went home and lay on the couch. My dad was watching TV from another couch in the same room. I heard the theme song to *Cheers* play. Ironically, *Cheers* is a song about life's hardships and having a place where you can go and everyone knows your name; you are accepted. And if you look up the meaning of "cheers," one meaning is "I trust you." I lost trust in the closest people around me. My heart was broken and tears streamed down my face. The pain grew both physically and emotionally. My dad was oblivious to all that was happening. Shortly thereafter, I went upstairs to bed and cried myself to sleep.

The next day, I was back at the abortion clinic. I only remember lying on the operating table hearing an obnoxious vacuum cleaner. The whole time, I was emotionally numbed inside while watching the clock in anticipation for it all to be over. The emotional pain still visits at times. Abortion gives birth to shame, guilt, and regret. These effects are true for men too. Abortion is not only a woman's issue. Men should feel free to speak out about their experiences with abortion. I hate abortion. I would not recommend it to my worst enemy.

> *"Abortion is the ultimate violence."*
> —Robert Casey, Sr.

MAKING SENSE OF IT ALL

After reading a portion of *Mindsight: The New Science of Personal Transformation* by Dr. Daniel J. Siegel, about "the narrative of dismissing adults," I believe that I fall into the category of a child who was dismissed by her parents. Many times, I felt alone and on my own. At times, I took on the role of a "little adult." This was premature autonomy playing out when I was left to cook dinner for my dad from scratch while my mom worked. Two things happened as a result: 1) I have been able to dismiss relationships easily during my younger, dating years. If things didn't work out in a relationship, I was quick to move on. I recognize that this mindset falls under the guise of dismissing adult attachment. 2) As an adult, autonomy is very important to me.

These patterns of attachment can be passed down from generation to generation. However, Dr. Siegel points to a crucial point: "When it comes to how our children will be attached to us, having difficult experiences early in life is less important than whether we've found a way to make sense of how those experiences have affected us. Making sense is a source of strength and resilience." In other words, when you work through your past, your future will be better. When you make a mistake, learn from it.

Stop and think for a moment what patterns of dysfunction there are in your family line. This can include addiction, abortion, domestic violence, molestation, etc. Pastor Larry Huch, author of *Free at Last*, also writes about the passing of things from generation to generation. I want to share with you an excerpt from his book:

> Matthew 24:12 tells us that not only will iniquity pass from generation to generation, but that iniquity will abound. That word "*abound*" is translated from the Greek word, *pluthuno*, which means "to increase." So not only does this force pass on from generation to generation, but it gets much worse in each generation.

I see what could be labeled as "generational curses" playing out in my family. I bring this information forward as a resource to aid in creating awareness for you. It's an interesting topic to consider. When you are consciously aware of the existence of such things, you can prevent them by the decisions you make. In other words, you can break the curse.

It is a rarity to learn from other's mistakes. Some people need to reach a threshold of pain first. I want to shine light on this truth to facilitate an awakening in people to prevent poor choices from occurring in the first place. This is why I'm sharing my story with you. I hope my story will aid you in making a decision you will not regret.

Until you become aware of something, you cannot change it. I observed things but did not give them attention. Communication and education from my parents would have been helpful; however, it still might not have been enough to prevent poor decisions. Has society not yet learned that education is not enough? Many years of sex education and drug education in the schools has not solved the issue of poor choice. Awareness and education mean nothing if kids do not know how to implement skills to make better choices using the information. The schools cannot take on the burden alone. As parents, you start the discussion and lead with your actions. What else is missing? It requires going beyond the surface.

BREAKING THE CURSE

All of the symptoms of dysfunction are on the surface. Going beyond the surface, beyond the presenting diagnosis, is to get to the root cause. We already know the effects on individuals and families. However, I believe there is a lack of understanding for how to fight against these familial atrocities. If you think about your life from a spiritual perspective, you can go beyond the surface to that which is not seen. A curse is something you only see through its effects. Battling in the spiritual realm is where victory is found. I believe you must fight against these curses through prayer. It is what is known as spiritual warfare. Here is where the true power resides. It is time to become knowledgeable in how this works and apply it. Remember, there is power in the tongue and there is power in prayer!

Pray for what you desire as if it has already happened. Give thanks for its outcome. Sometimes all you can hope and pray for is a miracle to happen.

HONOR, COURAGE, COMMITMENT

Life is precious. Your life is precious. If you were faced with a life and death situation, would you not do everything you could to continue to live? My mom made the decision to give me the gift of life. Life is celebrated every year through birthdays, milestones, and again at death. If life is so precious, why then do we continue as a society to throw it away as if it were an inanimate object? I'll tell you why: Because we don't even value ourselves! If we truly valued ourselves, we would value our life and the lives of others. *Inanimate objects don't grow hearts.*

Courage is what gives us strength to do the right thing even in the face of adversity. I wished I'd had the courage not to have that abortion. It has been a major regret in my life, and I share it so that if you or someone you know is ever in this situation, you know it is not something to be taken lightly. It was the most horrific, traumatic experience in my life. And it could have been *prevented* with birth control. Abortion will be something that impacts you and, potentially, the next generation of your family. Any time you experience a regret in life, you will inherit its effects. For me, it is depression.

Honor yourself and your values. Have courage to stand for the things you value even through adversity. Commit to living your life in alignment with the values that will bring honor to your life and your family.

Conviction That Produces Change

If you have already done as I have, you have my heartfelt condolences for your loss. There is hope for healing and self-forgiveness ahead of you. Take all of your regret, guilt, and shame and use it to prevent this pain from ever happening again.

Not long after the abortion, I discovered I was pregnant! Again! What was I going to do now? How would this work in the military? You would think that after having been through such a horrific experience, I would have learned my lesson and gone on birth control. I have no idea why birth control was not on my radar. But I knew one thing for certain—I could not and would not have another abortion. It was out of the question. I made my decision to have my baby. There was no doubt. I gave birth to a beautiful baby boy. I am so very thankful to God that I did not have a second abortion. I used my past painful experience to make a better decision.

SUMMARY

All families have muck that is passed down from generation to generation. Muck shows up in many forms: alcohol and drug addiction, abortion, children born out of wedlock, and divorce. These issues plague many families. Be aware and beware! If you recognize your family patterns and communicate with each other about them, you can *plan* to be consciously aware of your actions and decisions; then perhaps you can prevent hardship and pain for the next generation. Add prayer to your toolbox in fighting against these patterns.

Remember, if you find yourself entangled in a heaping mess, it isn't what you've gone through that is important—it's how you make sense of it. When you make sense of something, you get clear about it and have awareness, which then moves you forward. Understanding how your mistakes have affected you will facilitate change if you do the work. Learn from your mistakes and live consciously instead of by default. For me, I began to self-medicate my depression with alcohol. You can learn from your mistakes and save yourself from further injuring yourself. Reflection after a painful mistake is the first step in preventing it from happening again, but you must also commit to not allowing repeat regrets.

Because of my life experiences, I know that mine do not have to be repeated by others. I hope you will contemplate the decisions that will have life-impacting consequences. Reflect! Think! What is your heart telling you? This is a good place to start to look for the answer that is right for you.

I wish I would have listened to my heart and not aborted my first child. Had I decided to keep my baby, I believe

> REMEMBER, IF YOU FIND YOURSELF ENTANGLED IN A HEAPING MESS, IT ISN'T WHAT YOU'VE GONE THROUGH THAT IS IMPORTANT—IT'S HOW YOU MAKE SENSE OF IT.

resources and support would have come my way. I am not proud of this act, and I grieve my lost child. My wish for others is that they choose life for their unborn, regardless of the muck.

REFLECTION QUESTIONS

What has happened to you that had a profound impact on your life?

_____

_____

_____

_____

_____

_____

How has this decision personally impacted you?

_____

_____

_____

_____

_____

If you could live a life of no regrets, what decisions would you make?

_____

_____

_____

_____

_____

_____

What family patterns do you recognize?

_____

_____

_____

_____

_____

_____

What steps will you take to aid in making sense of it all?

_____

_____

_____

_____

_____

_____

What do you honor and commit to?

_____

_____

_____

_____

_____

_____

3

DIVORCING DOMESTIC VIOLENCE

*"Unless someone like you cares a whole awful lot,
nothing is going to get better. It's not."*

—Dr. Seuss

As I stated in the previous chapter, you can learn to break patterns and move forward consciously. Making sense out of your past helps you create a better future not only for yourself but also your children. When faced with making a decision that will impact your life forever, choose the answer that would leave you without regret. Think things through beyond the presenting situation or moment. How will this decision impact you in 5–10 years?

Let's take a look at marriage. Marriage is another example of a life-impacting decision people make on a regular basis and, perhaps, too lightly. Sometimes the excitement of a new relationship and the hope of a happily-ever after get in the way of seeing and accepting red flags that are signs of a marriage headed for doom. I've included a list of red flags at the end of this chapter to help you determine whether or not you should run or stay in the relationship. And even if you aren't contemplating marriage yet, this chapter may save you some grief later.

FEELING DESPERATE

Desperate people do desperate things. Six months into my pregnancy, my son's father told me he was married! There wasn't anything I could do to change that fact. Normally, this news would have been traumatic for someone to hear, but for me, it was another painful situation that I dismissed. I moved on and didn't let it faze me. To have the baby was never a question.

Even if he left his wife, I knew it would never work between us. I didn't want someone who had a heart for another woman. Plus, I figured he would cheat on me too. I felt badly for his wife and didn't want to cause any more harm to their marriage. I wasn't going to spend energy chasing after a man who wasn't mine.

When my son was born, I was living in San Diego as a young, single mother in the Navy. There was no family support near me. I was barely making it financially. As my son grew, I started to realize he deserved to have a dad. He had a dad, but under the circumstances, I had no expectation that he would be around. I wanted my son to feel the love of a father. I wanted to have a normal family. Being single and struggling to do it all alone was getting old. I wanted something better for my son.

MARRYING INTO THE MUCK

Soon after, I met a sailor. It was *lust* at first sight. He filled out a pair of Levi's 501 button fly jeans nicely. He looked like Ricky Bell from the band that started as New Edition and later became Bell Biv DeVoe. Somehow, his favoring Ricky Bell made my boyfriend all the more attractive to me. We had points of connection that made us seem like a good match—both from Illinois, both in the Navy, and we drove the same make and model car. (Really stupid points.) As the relationship progressed, the pressures of real life settled in and our drinking kept up with those pressures. Red flags were flying high, but I dismissed them without much conscious thought because my end goal was to get married and have a father for my baby.

We got married although none of our family attended the wedding. My new husband was taking on the role of dad for my son. We were in the honeymoon stage and life was changing fast. A move to Washington State through the Navy, married with a child, and another on the way! Like my other pregnancies, this was not planned. It felt right being newly married and going through the normal progression of building a family. My new world revolved around taking care of the boys and trying to be the homemaker while working in the Navy.

I tried to keep my husband happy and all of my efforts were never good enough. By trying to please him, I lost a part of me. Every time we had a blow up, I became a scared child again. Every time there was a verbal put-down or a physical fight, I lost confidence and self-worth. Eventually, I lost my total sense of self in this relationship. I was dying a subtle death because, little by little, the person I used to be was no longer around. My already low self-esteem sunk to new levels. At times throughout the marriage, I felt completely belittled, ridiculed, and taken advantage of physically, mentally, and financially.

MAKING SENSE OF IT ALL

Growing up in an alcoholic home meant we were certain of the uncertainty. When Dad pulled up in the driveway, one of us kids would yell, "Dad's home! Hurry up; change the channel!" We all scattered. One of us would put the channel to the news and the rest of us would run upstairs. We would try to be as quiet as possible and see whether he was going to yell for us to do something like get him a beer. Mom was at work. It was like walking on eggshells and being afraid to crack them.

Obviously, we didn't have the kind of relationship where we were excited to see him when he came home from work. When I was very little, I ran into his arms with joy. Then as I got older, the relationship changed. I wish our relationship had continued to grow in a healthy way, but instead, it became null and void.

Despite the "gun incident," there wasn't a great deal of physical violence in my home growing up. So how in the hell did I end up with an abusive husband? Reflecting on my childhood, I only remember being spanked once by my mom. My brother was the only one I recall getting in a couple of physical altercations with Dad, and that was because he was in trouble for doing stupid boy stuff. My dad could give me a certain look of disgust, and I would cower into myself or the nearest wall or corner. He would get up to get a beer, and if the cat happened to cross his path, he would try to give it a swift kick. And at the same time, he seemed pretty harmless. He worked hard, came home, cracked open a beer, and fell asleep. This was his pattern, his life.

For the most part, my family was merely cohabitating together without much conversation. It seemed best to be unseen and quiet. I don't recall much other than going to school, getting decent grades, and doing what I thought was expected of me. I noticed that my friends had a bedtime, but I never did; I gave myself a curfew to be home before dark; I was afraid of the dark anyway. It's no wonder all my life I've had a difficult time creating boundaries with alcohol, men, and my children—no one ever set any boundaries for me.

I see now the environment I grew up in was the same environment and even worse in marriage. My activities in my marriage revolved around keeping my husband happy while walking on eggshells. I never knew when he was going to start an argument, so I was always on guard. He would intentionally start an argument to give himself an excuse to leave and then go have affairs. As time went on, I could predict when the argument was coming. He was a womanizer, manipulator, and abuser. My dad also had affairs except he had no reason to pick a fight to leave because my mom was working at night. I never heard my dad put my mother down or lay a finger on her. Even after the affairs, my mom chose to stay in the marriage and until death did they part.

The common thread to all of this is the underlying emotional abuse that took place in my home growing up. There may not have been much physical abuse happening, but my dad's behaviors really set the stage for choosing an abusive partner; specifically, those behaviors were intimidation, yelling, cursing, name-calling (even if it was toward someone other than myself), and not giving a rip. He didn't spend time playing with me. I was ignored, even though I sat in the same room with him for hours on end.

Struggling to Leave

It wasn't until I started attending a domestic violence women's group through the Navy Family Advocacy Program that I really learned to recognize what domestic violence was and that there was an actual cycle to this beast. I would go to the group and gain knowledge, then come home and try to tell my husband what I had learned. BIG MISTAKE! He would be infuriated. I can only assume his anger was due to being confronted about his behaviors. He wasn't going to get away with his behaviors because as I gained knowledge and strength, my tolerance for abuse lessened. He would twist things until

I found myself getting angry with the counselor. True manipulation played out. This was crazy-making chaos in its finest form. He would make me think I was crazy and wrong. He turned me against the counselor.

When I stopped listening to him and started listening to the professionals, a shift occurred. Then I was able to identify domestic violence, no matter how subtle the abuse. I became less tolerant of his actions. I could predict when the next argument was coming. The physical abuse increased in severity as time passed. I learned, for my own safety, to have a plan of escape. How crazy is that? Here's an aha moment: *If I have to plan an escape from your ass, then I don't need to be with you!*

I was distraught at times, and I opened up to my coworkers and friends at the time. It is so important to speak up and talk about your situation. Too often, a victim remains silent out of fear or due to shame. Coworkers began to refer to my husband as "Dr. Jekyll and Mr. Hyde." He would act one way in front of people and another way in his home. I questioned what God would want for me in this situation and thought I was obligated to the covenant of marriage. A friend clarified the biblical aspects of this situation and told me, "God does not say to be a doormat." The way she explained it was that domestic violence is a breach in the covenant that makes divorce permissible.

I wanted to break the cycle and the curse of domestic violence for my children. Quite honestly, I didn't have the self-esteem to get out of this relationship for my own sake. But I valued my children more than myself, so I got out for them. The irony is often we feel we need to *stay* because of the children, but when all attempts to correct the behaviors fail, you really need to *leave* for the children!

> THE IRONY IS OFTEN WE FEEL WE NEED TO STAY BECAUSE OF THE CHILDREN, BUT WHEN ALL ATTEMPTS TO CORRECT THE BEHAVIORS FAIL, YOU REALLY NEED TO LEAVE FOR THE CHILDREN!

It took me seven years of marriage and a painful physical injury before I concluded that staying was not an option. Everyone has a pain threshold, a breaking point. Mine was a cracked rib! If this man could crack my rib while my family was visiting from out of state, then what would he do when they weren't around? The physical injuries were becoming more severe.

My ego screwed with me throughout this process. I felt like a complete failure. I had failed at marriage and I had failed my children. At least that was how I felt in the moment. The greater realization came when I thought about my kids and the impact the marriage would have on them. I didn't want my children to repeat the pattern of domestic violence. I did not want my sons to be addicted to pornography or to abuse women—both activities they could learn from their father if I remained with him.

Many things led up to my leaving. Here are a few: Listening to others around me, getting professional help from counselors, and learning more about my husband's upbringing. They all shed light on how serious this really could become. He was also not willing to change and seek help for himself.

What is important here is that I got out of the situation and was able to gain the strength and courage to find peace. I got out for the safety and wellbeing of my kids and myself.

Getting Help

It wasn't until I reached my threshold of pain that I was ready to leave for good. Realizing the impact this living environment would have on my kids was a significant factor in me leaving the marriage after seven years. I did not want my boys to grow up treating women the way I was treated. I did not want my boys to grow up thinking abuse was okay or the norm.

Almost twenty years ago, I was given a picture of a Power and Control Wheel showing the cycle of domestic violence.

It is still relevant today. The wheel is based on a male dominating the relationship with a woman. If I were to update the wheel, I would definitely change it to be gender neutral. Domestic violence does not discriminate; all people regardless of gender or ethnicity fall prey to violence. I am not the expert so I will refer you to the website for the wheel's creators: http://www.theduluthmodel.org. Due to copyrights, I am not able to provide the wheel here. It is worth looking up.

SUMMARY

Domestic violence will not go away in our lifetimes. If it happens to you, you must protect your children and get help. Speak up and seek help. I know it isn't easy to talk about it. Whenever I would share what happened with a friend, I would shake and fill with anxiety. It took a toll on my nervous system. Regardless, how difficult it may be in the moment, you must tell someone. I personally know people whose lives have been dramatically changed by domestic violence. In one case, the perpetrator killed his wife. In the other case, I know a girl whose mother was killed by her stepfather when she was twelve, leaving her to care for her younger siblings. Domestic violence is a serious issue that can lead to death. One time is too many. Do not listen to the abuser. Listen to the professionals. The professionals have seen this story play out over and over again. You are the same character in the story except with a different name. How many times will you let this story play out in your life?

You deserve to be safe. Your kids deserve to live in a home filled with love and peace. There is nothing wrong with you. You are not crazy although you may feel like it at times. You can get out, and you can make it in life! There is hope for a better day. Be courageous and move forward wisely through this situation with the help of professionals. You do not deserve to be hit, slapped, kicked, raped, or strangled. You are worth every fiber of your being. If you can't do it for yourself, then do it for your children! They do not deserve nor desire to see their mommy or daddy hurt, injured, and crying. Demonstrate for your children what it looks like to seek help in adversity. Demonstrate for your children what it is to value yourself so they will value themselves.

You have a story to tell that will help others. You won't be able to help others and make a difference if you don't get out. Get out and live to tell your story!

REFLECTION QUESTIONS

What environment did you grow up in?

_____

_____

_____

_____

_____

_____

What red flags do you see in your relationship?

_____

_____

_____

_____

_____

_____

What altercations have you had with your significant other?

_____

_____

_____

_____

_____

_____

What is the impact of this environment on your children?

_____
_____
_____
_____
_____
_____

Are you ready to value yourself and your children enough to get out?

_____
_____
_____
_____
_____
_____

What is your safety plan?

_____
_____
_____
_____
_____

TOP FIVE RED FLAGS

Any one of these would be enough and good reason to say, "Muck Off!"

1) Physical altercations: slap, kick, punch, any form of unwanted physical touch to include tickling.

2) Verbal Abuse: Name calling, asking you to change the way you dress or to change your makeup. Making fun of the way you look.

3) Controlling whom you talk to and prohibiting you from seeing family and friends. Very jealous of others in your circle.

4) Lack of commitment to the relationship. Having sex with others even though the expectation for you is to refrain from having sex with others.

5) Family history: What did your significant other witness growing up?

Red flags ignite our intuition. We know deep inside something is not right. Do not ignore them and listen to your intuition. You will save yourself years of grief.

An encouraging word:

"Be strong and of good courage, do not fear nor be afraid of them; for the Lord your God, He is the One who goes with you. He will not leave you nor forsake you."
—Deuteronomy 31:6 (New King James Version)

4

PLAYING THE PLAYER

"Every flower grows in dirt."

—Anonymous

You've learned you have a decision to make if you are in an abusive relationship. You either stay (if you are safe) *and* both individuals work on the relationship *and* you work on yourselves as individuals, *or* you leave. Those are the only two choices; otherwise, you get stuck on the merry-go-round of insanity with more chaos and the consequences of staying—which could be an early death.

My behaviors before my marriage and after my divorce were the same. I reverted back to "playing the field." My objective for playing the field was to find my prince. However, my opponents who were playing along had their own objective: merely to have a good time with the added benefit of sex. Someone who takes advantage of another with no intention of building a serious relationship is the definition of a "player." It doesn't take long to know whether a relationship is moving forward or whether it is serving another purpose. How much time are you willing to waste on a dead-end relationship? My mistake was putting the cart (sex) before the horse (relationship).

I didn't want to be that girl with the reputation of being easy. I wanted to be loved and valued. I couldn't get those things from another person until I learned to love and value myself. Promiscuity is a by-product of low self-esteem. When you participate in these behaviors, you aren't valuing yourself or your body. Living this lifestyle brings forth lust.

Recognizing Lust

Lust is the intense desire to have sex, and its behavior is promiscuity. Now add the use of alcohol. With alcohol, you lose self-control and inhibition. It's as if they go hand-in-hand almost as if they are co-dependent upon each other. Promiscuous behaviors and alcohol created almost all of the muck in my life. Living a promiscuous life left me chasing after men, feeling empty and broken-hearted.

How do you recognize lust in your life? It starts with an attraction that goes beyond boundaries to having sex with someone whether you know the person or not. It's as if you drink a "love" potion, and you are now under a spell. It feels like a negative force that makes you feel like you have no self-control. You become a siren calling out to men and attracting the wrong type of men. Before you know it, you're in bed with this person. Gross. Lust takes you captive and follows you everywhere; work, college, grocery store, etc. It is a stronghold.

> WHEN I STARTED ANALYZING WHAT I WAS DOING, I REALIZED ALL OF THESE MEN DRESSED THE SAME, ACTED THE SAME, AND WERE VERY SIMILAR TO EACH OTHER.

Going from "relationship" to "relationship" meant I was rebounding from one man to another. When I started analyzing what I was doing, I realized all of these men dressed the same, acted the same, and were very similar to each other. They were charismatic, independent, self-sufficient bachelors who liked to drink. I describe them as players because that's what they did—they played with several women at a time. These men were unable to commit to a monogamous relationship or they had no reason to commit because they were getting what they wanted from me without the commitment.

Sex does not equal love, but the act itself will provide "faux love"—a false feeling of being loved. It's a Band-Aid for the low self-esteem. Using alcohol and sex was a great distraction from the pain I needed to uncover and resolve. Lust, as with anything else, doesn't go away until you deal with it.

Eventually, my view of men became tainted. I thought men had no hearts. I decided to guard my heart and continue the game. I was getting better at playing it too. If I wasn't called by Wednesday, I was unavailable for the weekend. This was a boundary. As small and silly as it may seem, it was teaching me to be unavailable and put myself first. I was starting to value myself. It was slowing myself down and putting a pause in place. Very slowly, I got fed up with being the party girl. I was trying to win the game of cat and mouse without a strategy. My way wasn't working.

COMBATING LUST

Think about how lust affects your relationships. It isn't something you want following you into marriage or any relationship for that matter. There is a physical and spiritual way to combat lust. Unless you are supernaturally healed of it by God, I recommend taking the following steps in the right direction. First, remove yourself from what is holding you back. Abstain, at least for a period of exploration, from any mind-altering substances. Abstain from pornography and any behaviors along this line. Porn is mind-altering. Abstain from sex. Both pornography and sex hinder progress. You are cleansing the environment to make space for something new.

*"Therefore let us not sleep, as [do] others; but let us
watch and be sober."*
—1 Thessalonians 5:6 (New King James Version)

Then begin to do a deep dive on your relationships. What patterns do you see? What type of person do you continuously choose? By taking time out and being alone, you can break these patterns of attracting people who aren't working for you. Look at the patterns in your own family. Have there been affairs? What has been their impact? How has lust played out in your family?

Get to the core of the issue by working on your self-esteem. This work involves reflecting on your childhood. Where did your lack of self-worth first begin? Read self-help books in this area. Get professional counseling. God gave you a brain, so use it and get the help you need.

Get clear on whom you want to be and whom you want in a spouse. Ask God, in your own simple way, to remove the stronghold of lust and to give you a new set of eyes. Thank God in advance for giving you self-worth and new eyesight. Praying is the simplest thing you can do, and God expects you to take action.

Safeguarding Your Success

All of the work above does not happen overnight. It is a process so it takes time to do the work. While you are doing your work, God is doing His work. When you finally arrive at your destination, how will you keep moving forward? Hopefully, you've gotten to the root of the matter and really worked on your self-esteem.

Life has a way of knocking you down when you least expect it. Something may happen in life that puts you in a vulnerable state. When you feel like crap on the inside, behaviors show up on the outside. When your needs aren't getting met, it isn't an excuse to freak out. These are the times when you need to proceed with caution. Knowing yourself well enough to know how you behave in these times of being under pressure, stress, and vulnerability will help prevent you from getting dirty again. Learning different coping skills that work for you during these times is necessary. The behaviors you normally fall back on during stressful times—such as drugs, alcohol, sex—are no longer an option. Stretch yourself to go deeper and analyze your own behaviors. It took me a long time to grow up and stop playing in the dirt. I'm still growing, except not from dirt. I'm growing from positive experiences and people.

Once I overcame lust, I recognized a change in me. Now, an attractive man is no longer an object of lust for me; I can look at a man and think he is attractive, but that's where it ends. I can see that he is someone I would have lusted over in the past, but now I see him with new eyes. God has delivered me from this snare.

SUMMARY

The cycle of domestic violence must be broken, and I had to break the cycle of attracting men who were not for me. Changing my behaviors and becoming the person I needed to be was required to attract the right man for me. After living a promiscuous life and understanding it was rooted in low self-esteem, I gradually woke up to what I truly wanted in myself and a life partner.

Lust mixed with alcohol is a recipe for self-destruction and a broken heart. Combating lust requires physical and spiritual action. You create the space necessary to bring in your prince by cleaning up your behaviors that are not serving you. Admit that your way is not working!

To achieve self-esteem, you need to identify those things that stripped you of your value and sense of worth. Then work on rebuilding your value by creating boundaries, ceasing self-defeating behaviors, and not allowing what you don't want in your life. Game over. Stop playing in the dirt.

Simply ask God to deliver you from lust and thank Him, in advance, for giving you self-worth and new eyesight to see the opposite sex through a new lens. Your overall objective changes from chasing after the wrong man to becoming someone who values him- or herself enough to choose differently.

REFLECTION QUESTIONS

How much time are you willing to waste on a dead-end relationship?

_____

_____

_____

_____

_____

_____

What behaviors do you need to change?

_____

_____

_____

_____

_____

_____

What boundaries will you create to move you forward?

_____

_____

_____

_____

_____

_____

What character traits do you want to adopt as your own?

_____

_____

_____

_____

_____

_____

What character traits do you want in a partner?

_____

_____

_____

_____

_____

_____

SUMMARY OF SECTION ONE: REFLECT

Reflection is an important step in moving forward. Sometimes you need to take a step back to take two steps forward. By looking back, you begin to create awareness of where your healing process begins. Reflection allows you to identify the root cause of your behaviors. You start to see the effect of your choices and behaviors.

If you've been answering the questions at the end of each chapter, you've already begun to reflect. Take a moment in a quiet place to be all alone with your journal. Breathe deeply and feel the ground under your feet. Clear your mind. Think about the most significant events of your life. Even if you jot down a bulleted list of those experiences, it is a start. Now think about your last year. What stands out? What has changed in your life from years gone by? And finally, reflect on yesterday. Does your yesterday reflect the life you want to be living?

Make a commitment to journal once a day or once a week as a way to reflect. Journaling is a fantastic tool I use to reflect.

You may find having separate journals for specific topics is useful. For example, one journal for business ideas, another for remembering all you are grateful for, and another for getting everything out. Take fifteen minutes a day or week and journal. Get your thoughts on paper. As you do this exercise, think about the decisions you've made, the impact they had on you and your loved ones, and the challenge you are living now.

When you go through the *motions,* you rarely have a profound realization. When you do what society dictates you *should* do—go to work, pay bills, and do it all over again; day after day, month after month, year after year—what is the point of it all? Today's fast-paced society has created the walking dead. Zombies on autopilot move about the day without intent. Slow down, reflect, and start creating the person you were meant to be. Start creating the life you deserve!

If you find yourself in any of the situations I have been in, seek help! I know this sounds so obvious, yet so many people never get the help they need, so their lives stay stuck in the muck. Nothing changes, and then life is over. Get counseling, read self-help books, partner with a coach, and learn to be alone with yourself. Turn off your cell phone and focus on you. Take the time to learn about yourself and stop the destructive patterns. *Make sense of yourself—that is where you discover that knowledge is power.* The knowledge you gain you can apply to achieve a healthy life.

SECTION TWO

RECOVER

I WANT TO BE TREATED LIKE A PERSON,
NOT A PRINCESS!

Upon looking in the mirror again and realizing what was there, this princess decided to take back that part of her that was once left behind. This princess had the courage to face the pain, and she wept and wept some more. Then she started to feel better. She started to recover her broken heart. She wanted so much more for her life. She learned how to persevere and love herself. She was able to dream again.

Section Two focuses on the process of recovery. Different perspectives of what recovery may look like are presented. This section is meant to get you thinking about your recovery and what the recovery plan for you should look like because you know best what you are willing to do for yourself. Change starts with you, and no one else can do the work for you. Recovery takes time. Make it a priority and see what happens. What you focus on is where you will see your results.

5

SEEKING RECOVERY

Reflection has a way of digging up old wounds, memories, and emotions. You may find guilt, regret, and depression try to get the best of you. Be aware of these emotions and allow them to surface. Embrace them and know you are entering into recovery. Recovery is a process that starts with courage and ends with healing your heart. By bringing these things to the surface and dealing with them, you begin to heal.

When you get to the root of emotion, the behaviors that keep you stuck will dissolve like a melting ice cube. These are the self-sabotaging, self-destructive behaviors connected to an area that needs healing. When you identify behaviors, and get to the root of the emotion causing the behaviors, you demolish them!

Unless you deal with something, it does not go away. Not only does it stick around; it creates other consequences.

Consider your bills, for example. They do not go away until you do something with them. You may even pay a late fee. A late fee may be the passing down of these mistakes to the next generation. That's a hefty late fee!

On the brighter side, reflection creates the space to remember the parts of yourself that you wish to bring back to life. If you truly want permanent change, it starts with recovery.

WELCOME TO RECOVERY

Recovery is the term used to describe the process of healing from the past. Maybe something just happened yesterday; it is still in the past. Through the process of recovery, you are healing your wounds, whether they be physical or emotional. As with an open wound, it takes time. During recovery, you feel pain as if you're cleaning shards of glass from a wound. Eventually, the pain subsides and new growth comes through introspection, forgiveness, and self-development. Once you are healed, you are ready to live life to the fullest. You feel like yourself again. You are free from those emotions that kept you from experiencing joy. Your heart is beating again.

Whatever mistakes you've made or pain you have endured, it is time to let go! You should feel a little excited—actually, you should be exploding with excitement for the life you are about to create! You are going to be the very best version of you. Imagine the possibilities of how you can feel, look, and enjoy *you*. The *real* you. Even though you've faced all sorts of adversity, you can take it and turn it into something so beautiful.

Whatever tears you down and goes against where you want to be is what you will remove and replace with what you do want in your life. Whatever takes away from you being you is where you can start your focus. Often, this is where you will find meaning for your life. You serve others by helping them with the very thing you've recovered from and the possibilities are endless.

STARTING YOUR RECOVERY MISSION

What's the first thing you do when you lose something? You think back to when you last saw it. You trace your steps back in an effort to find what you lost. Once you find it, you move forward in your day. This is exactly what happens in recovery. At some point in your life, you lost a part of yourself. Your heart was broken. You might think you've gotten over something, but the emotion keeps showing up in your life. The event is over, and that emotion you felt is now a pattern showing up in your career, relationships, etc. Your feelings of depression, guilt, shame, and regret are affecting your life. You lack confidence and never feel like you are good enough. Regardless of your emotions and symptoms, you need to trace your steps back to when you first started feeling the way you do. Analyze how each emotion is creeping into your daily life.

Recovery at the core is the healing of your heart. Without a properly functioning heart, you are unable to enjoy life at full capacity. Perhaps you've heard the saying, "Hurt people, hurt people." The deep hurt in one person calls out to the hurt in another person. Instead of

> RECOVERY AT THE CORE IS THE HEALING OF YOUR HEART.

pointing fingers, figure out what it is in you that attracted you to that person. The healing you do restores your life. You make new choices for yourself. You are able to go after your dreams. Without recovery, there is no blood flow; when there is no blood flow, people die. Dreams die. Mistakes are repeated and then passed down. This is why it is so important to seek recovery.

Let's get your heart pumping and working at full capacity. You are hereby commissioned to the mission of healing your heart. Full restoration of your heart is in order. You are on a very important mission.

Opening Your Heart

Heart surgery requires an open heart. No matter how small the incision, there is an opening that allows instruments in to stabilize the patient's condition. You can breathe.

It is a requirement for you to open your heart to allow healing in. A hardened heart is hard, like a baseball; nothing comes in and nothing goes out. Make the decision to be willing to soften your heart. Allow yourself to be vulnerable in order to clean out the negative feelings. You can do this in a safe environment with a professional or in your own home by yourself.

Resuscitating Your Life

Lay on the ground as if you have had a heart attack. I'm serious. Get on the floor! Your life has literally just stopped. This is a "timeout" from life. If you were really on your deathbed, you'd have no choice. Don't give yourself a choice (an excuse) not to perform this surgery that will save your life. Your family is counting on you to get this surgery. Allow yourself the timeout. You are not being selfish. In fact, you are not only giving yourself the gift of healing, but you are demonstrating self-care to those around you. You are going to come out on the other side beaming with joy. This is what your family and friends want for you.

Imagine the paramedics kneeling around you. Your shirt has been cut away.

You are moving back and forth between consciousness and unconsciousness. Your life is flashing in front of you. You remember the list of events in your life that caused great pain. This pain has clogged your arteries and cut off the blood from flowing freely. What is the first event that comes to mind? This experience is where your recovery starts.

What emotion is connected to this event? How does this emotion show up in your career, relationships, conversations, daily life? Journal your answers. (If you're still on the floor, please feel free to get up.) Emotions that are tied to an event will continue to show up as a pattern in your life until you go back to the place of hurt where you acquired them.

Anger was an emotion that was showing up for me, and I didn't understand why or where it was coming from. It was coming with me into my work and general conversations. I asked myself, "Why am I so damned angry?" In a dream, my dad's face showed up. I thought I had forgiven him, but I needed to revisit our relationship. My dad had died more than twenty years earlier, but the emotions of the traumatic gun incident and abandonment were still there at the subconscious level. I had some work to do.

You've identified the entry point of recovery. This is a huge step. Big hugs. Like a surgeon's steady hands, continue slowly. Be gentle with yourself. You are the patient.

STEPS TO RECOVERY

After all of the muck I have been through, some key elements have risen to the top of my list that aided in my recovery. What does recovery mean? To me, it means getting to the state where I can think clearly and move forward. A certain amount of healing has occurred, so I can talk about the situation without getting caught up in emotion. I am restored to the place of wholeness, capability, creativity, and resourcefulness. I am able to move forward.

The following list of items helped me get back on track during difficult times:

1) **Knowledge:** Gather facts and data to better understand the situation, disease, or root cause.

2) **Reflection:** What did I learn? What is in my control to change? What am I choosing to change? What is most important to me?

3) Prayer: Ask God for what you need in a situation, or ask Him to change you and your feelings about it and your response.

4) Forgiveness: Forgive those who hurt you and keep a clean heart. Forgiving is not always easy, but in the end, forgiveness is for you, not the perpetrator. Admit when you are wrong and ask for forgiveness. Forgive yourself! This is probably more difficult than forgiving another person. Know that you are human, and in order to help someone else, you must forgive yourself. Forgiveness is so important. Chapter 7 spells it out.

5) Support: Seek support; whether it is a formal support organization, informal group, or a trusted family member or friend. In my opinion, professional help versus venting to a friend is best. Your friend is exhausted from listening to your broken record! (Your friend can thank me later for telling you this!)

6) Action: What's next? Look forward to your vision and do not dwell in the past. Take baby steps to get to the next step and keep on steppin'! Do something!

I firmly believe that with God all things are possible. It's up to you to create a recovery process for yourself that works. When it comes to recovery, one size does not fit all. You are unique and, therefore, your recovery process is unique. You know yourself best and what you need to do for yourself. This is self-help: educating yourself and following through with action. You are not codependent on any person or program, and instead, become confident in knowing yourself and what works for you. I'm not saying you will not utilize people or programs. I am saying you will get what you need from them and then move on to the next phase.

It's like counseling in that a good counselor will recognize whether the counseling sessions have served their purpose. You aren't going to go to a counselor consistently for the rest of your life, are you? No, only for a season. You decide the length of the season. For some, this season lasts a lifetime. Whatever works for you is what you know you need to do. Often you know what you need to do, but you don't do it. Other times, you go back and forth until you reach your threshold of pain and decide, once and for all, you will not go back. If you are in a recovery program, you belong there. You are right where you need to be. Don't get it twisted. I am not giving you permission to walk away from your program! Whatever "program" you are in, it's one procedure in the overall process of heart surgery.

Recovery is like being a lifelong learner. As long as you have breath, there are events, experiences, and circumstances that require recovery. Seeking recovery is not about a program, but rather providing a continuous source of fresh oxygen to aid you in living the very best you. *You don't recover because of how many days you attend a program. You recover because you do the work internally to get to the root cause of your pain.* It's the most liberating, empowering act of self-love you can do.

BEING THE BEST PATIENT EVER

As a patient, you understand the outcomes of not following the routine, prescriptions, and counsel. Likewise, you understand the risk involved of not following the procedure. Being the best patient ever means you stay persistent with the process, even while you are in pain. You can't stand the pain any longer and you finally stop complaining about it and seek help. You become your own best advocate. Now that you've identified the root of your pain, you know where to start. In the next chapter, I will give you tools to remain persistent and persevere.

SUMMARY

Transformation from the inside is the heart of recovery. Recovery starts with courage and ends with healing your heart. You must intentionally open your heart to allow healing. There was an event in your life that caused emotional pain, and this pain is showing up in areas of your life through emotion. By getting to the root cause of this emotion and working through it, you release this pain. You recover your sense of self and your heart beats again.

Reflecting allows you to go back to the place where you lost your sense of self. You open this wound so you can remove what is not serving you. Healing takes time, and you work through your process at your pace. You are determined to heal and reclaim yourself and your vision.

Your recovery is all about you. You are unique and your recovery is unique. You know yourself best. You already know what you are willing to do and what you are not willing to do. It's up to you to figure out what will work for you. You are your own best advocate. By becoming your own best advocate, you research and educate yourself on *you*. Figure out why you do what you do. Through this process, you identify lessons learned, what's most important to you, and what you choose to change. Limiting beliefs and self-sabotaging behaviors are replaced with empowering thoughts and behaviors that serve your vision. By getting to the root cause, you free yourself from the emotional pain that is keeping you from your vision.

Recovery is not a program. You don't recover because of how many days you attend a program. You recover because you do the work internally to get to the root cause of your pain. It's the most liberating, empowering act of self-love you can do. Giving yourself a timeout to do this work is so important for you.

A holistic approach to recovery—mind, body, soul—brings balance to your life. Learning about yourself, asking God for help, forgiving yourself and others, and seeking support from professionals is all part of your recovery. It requires action from you. *You own your recovery*. You create the vision for your life. There is support for you when you need it. You are not alone. You have to want this more than the people around you want it for you. You will love yourself for it.

You are no longer talking about what you are going to do. You are doing it. You are so tired of this pain that you are willing to let it go. Remember, if you take no action, you will remain in the same place where you started. The consequences of not doing the work are far worse than facing the pain now. Give yourself the gift of healing.

Let's move forward and get clear on what your vision of your happily ever after is. The next chapter provides perspective and tools to persevere on your journey.

Recovery Exercise

What event in your life has caused pain?

_____

_____

_____

_____

_____

_____

_____

_____

_____

_____

_____

_____

_____

_____

What emotion do you recognize from this event?

_____

_____

_____

_____

_____

_____

How is this emotion showing up in your life? (Do you see a pattern of this emotion in your relationships, career, or parenting?)

_____

_____

_____

_____

_____

_____

_____

_____

_____

What part of yourself did you lose?

_____

_____

_____

_____

_____

_____

_____

_____

_____

What are you willing to do to get that part of you back?

I understand this work is emotional and feels painful. I acknowledge you for your courage and strength to continue. It gets better, I promise. *Treat yourself to something nice today. You deserve it.*

6

PERSEVERING WHILE IN PROCESS

"The flower that blooms in adversity is the rarest and most beautiful of all."

—Walt Disney Company

The reality is you've spent your life taking care of others, or others have taken care of you to a fault. Somewhere, you lost sight of yourself and the things you've wanted to do in life. Up until now, you've taken in messages, labels, experiences, and environments that have shaped you. Some of these things have harmed you instead of helped you. Most of your life has been spent living with thoughts and behaviors that have not served you in a positive way. Because you've lived this way for so long, it's going to take some time to think differently and create new habits and behaviors.

If you completed the questions at the end of the last chapter, you have experienced what this work feels like at the beginning stages. I will be brutally honest with you. It is not for the weak. It takes time, effort, and perseverance. This is not a quick fix. The benefit of doing the work outweighs the alternative of not doing it. Relax; not all of the work is emotionally daunting. Eventually, it becomes fun, especially when you start living and feeling differently.

It's an investment in yourself, and you are well worth it! It's your time now. If you truly want to recover yourself, here's what you'll need. . . .

COURAGE

"Decision is a risk rooted in the courage of being free."
—Paul Tillich

Everything starts with a decision. Decide you want to change—people say they want to change and then do nothing. It takes a lot of courage to do something different from what you are comfortable doing. Reading this shows that you are seeking answers and have a desire to change something in your life. You might not make the connection between courage and reading a book. While the act itself may not require courage, the internal growth that comes along with it is very courageous. To persevere, you will need courage *repeatedly*.

Fear is what gets in the way of being courageous. By facing your fear, you move forward and prevent becoming paralyzed by it. The more you face difficult situations head-on, the more courage you obtain. Fear results from a *perceived* threat. Fear is often about something in the future or something unknown. My mind is very talented at perceiving threats. These are not real; they're only part of the story I've told myself. The circumstances of what "could" happen or the "what ifs" are part of your story. When the fear of not changing becomes greater than the fear itself, you will move forward. Stop here for a moment. Close your eyes and think of something you fear. Imagine the fear being gone. What do you see now? How do

> WHEN THE FEAR OF NOT CHANGING BECOMES GREATER THAN THE FEAR ITSELF, YOU WILL MOVE FORWARD.

you feel? I have learned to dismiss these thoughts and thank God in the moment for what I truly want to happen as if my prayer has already been answered. Create a new story for what you want and focus on it instead.

When you are presented with a real threat, fear can be used to your advantage to bring forth the courage necessary in the moment to defend yourself. However, the fear that builds up in your mind (not a real threat) is an obstacle to achieving your true self. This fear is something you conjure up all on your own. It is only as true as you allow it to be.

When you think about fear and realize it is an emotion, you can label it as a noun instead of a verb. It then becomes an object with no power. When it is a verb, it is in action, and to have an item in action takes energy. Fear exudes negative energy. This energy keeps you away from focusing on the thing you truly want and, in fact, it creates a negative reality. What you give your attention to is what you will manifest. Manifest the positive. Stay away from the negative energy.

Learning to push through negative feelings takes conscious awareness and effort. To practice something means to do it over and over. Practice replacing the negative with the positive. As you push through this exercise, you will grow in confidence and faith. Fear has a way of sneaking up at times. Battling fear requires you to become like a ninja and kick it in the butt by pulling out your weapon of faith. Faith in the simplest form, is believing. Using this weapon repeatedly makes you resilient. The more you practice recognizing and combating fear, the better you get at it. You begin to believe with your whole heart in the positive outcome of your desires. You've already succeeded in areas of your life, so why wouldn't you succeed now? As you grow in strength, courage, and faith, you become fearless!

RESILIENCE

Over the years, people have told me I'm strong. What exactly does that mean? To paraphrase an old wristwatch commercial, I "took a lickin' and kept on tickin'." Resilient is probably a better word. No matter what, I made it through. After stumbling or falling, I got back up and kept on going. My determination to change, and the belief it could happen, gave me courage and resulted in my being resilient.

Change is constant and obstacles will come. Unexpected events will occur for better or worse. You will get knocked down, but the important thing is to get back up. At times, you'll feel like it's really difficult. The faster you learn to get back up, the stronger you become. Keep assessing yourself and the situation and make changes when necessary. Being resilient means you are in motion. Even if you are working through the emotion, you are still in motion. You will make it through. You will persevere through one thing to the next. If you aren't moving, you become stagnant. Being stagnant puts you at risk of becoming too comfortable. You don't want to get stuck in complacency. Continue taking baby steps until you are back up to par. Keep going, even when you feel defeated.

SHOW UP

Showing up puts you in motion. This means you are shifting your current state into your future state. Every small action moves you either toward your goal or away from your goal. When you put yourself into action, change happens. Sometimes it's necessary to take a step back before moving forward. The point is to keep moving. Keep showing up for yourself; keep working on yourself. Keep showing up for your appointments, meetings, seminars, workshops, sessions, and classes.

I've learned to show up even if I didn't feel like it. Ever want to stay home from school because your assignment wasn't completed? Go anyway. You never know what will happen. Your instructor might extend the due date on the assignment. This happened to me. I went regardless because I needed to stay current on the content and get the brownie points for showing up.

Another example, the times I didn't feel like going to church but did anyway, were the times it was as if God were speaking directly to me. It's those times I pushed myself to go when I didn't want to that I grew the most. There seemed to be something extra special for me each time. No matter what, show up. You'll be happy you did.

Being consistent in showing up creates the rhythm to gain momentum. If you are going to half-ass it, then why bother? Half-assing it, is a waste of everyone's time and energy. *Life is too short to half-ass your dream.* In order for something to be effective, you must do it consistently. It's like taking medicine. You must take it on a regular basis in order for it to work. Some prescriptions tell you what time of day to take it. Be on time. Respect yourself enough to be on time. Show yourself you are committed. Implementing the habit of showing up and being on time is action toward valuing yourself.

Things in life come up, but not completing assignments is a lack of motivation, disorganization, or commitment. Or are you letting fear get in the way? This is a great time to push through with faith and trust the process. Of course, there are things that knock us off track, but these things are few and far between. For the most part, there are no excuses. Excuses only put you two steps behind. Going even deeper, it's a lack of self-worth.

The way to commit to something is to understand the value behind what you are doing. Some refer to this as "your why." When you find a good enough reason to do something, the reason will fuel your drive to get it done. Your "why" needs to be strong enough to sustain your drive. The reason behind what you do is for a purpose much greater than yourself. It's the big picture. It's your cause, your purpose. It is your mission in life that brings forth passion. This passion is what pumps the blood through your heart. This passion gets you bursting with energy and excitement. If you aren't excited, then your reason isn't great enough. You may need some initial healing and personal care first to clear the path in finding your passion.

PERSONAL CARE

Society dictates that going to work is something you *have to* do. At times, going to work brought relief because it was an escape from my own drama and chaos. It was one place where I felt normal again. Other times, I would have been better off not going to work so I could take care of myself. You'll need to decide what is best for you in certain situations. If you are the type of person who constantly pushes yourself when your world is falling apart, *force yourself to take time for you.*

You aren't shock resistant, and you don't have an unbreakable main spring. Despite going through one personal crisis after another, I still went to work. People around me knew what was going on and couldn't believe I was at work. Being independent and responsible all of my life, I felt I *had to* go to work. It's something you do regardless of what else is happening in your life. Realistically, I was on autopilot. My emotions, thoughts, and actions were compartmentalized. These three components—emotions, thoughts, and actions—were lumped together in separate boxes. If I was at work, I was able to focus and pull from my work compartment. If I was at home, all of my attention was coming from my home compartment. This is true for the major events in my life. Each event has a compartment. All of my emotions were suppressed into these compartments.

Compartments have only a certain amount of space, like a closet full of clothes that needs to be sorted through and purged of old clothes. When you get rid of clothes because they no longer fit with who you want to be, you create space for the new self you are to become. Open up the compartments where you've stuffed your emotions and thoughts. Purge the ones that no longer serve you. Someone like me, who has suppressed a lot of emotions over the years, may need to learn to cry again. It's freeing to release all of the muck I've been carrying around with me.

To remain resilient through the work you are about to do, make a plan for self-care. Decide what you are willing to do for yourself to maintain balance. This is so important to stay on track. Otherwise, getting caught up in the muck and losing focus on your vision will happen. When you are taking care of yourself, you cope better and feel better.

When you are stressed out, you stop doing the things you love most. This is the time when you need to continue to do those things that bring you joy, balance, and positive energy. Instead of "relapsing" into your typical stress-relieving behaviors, adopt new habits for coping. Choose healthy foods not the proverbial comfort foods. A little 80 percent cocoa dark chocolate is considered healthy, at least healthier than most other sugar options. A little chocolate goes a long way.

Keep your body in motion—dance, swim, hike, work out. Try a new physical activity. If you get off track, know that the longer you stay off track, the harder it is to get back on track. *Hit the reset button immediately.* The more you do this, the more you persevere. And the easier it gets.

Create a routine that allows time for you. Quality time to be with yourself and your emotions. Connect to yourself, your emotions, your soul.

PERSPECTIVE

Persevering is getting beyond the obstacle. When obstacles come, decide ahead of time that nothing is going to stop you. One big annoying obstacle came my way when I was close to being finished with this book. It was a sunny day and I sat out on my deck, ready to begin my work. I inserted the disc where this book was stored. After I clicked, File – Open, "The file is corrupt and cannot be opened" appeared on my screen. I could not believe my eyes. I tried to open the file again and again. Insanity was playing out. Hahaha. I went to the mall to see a Microsoft technician. He tried to retrieve and restore the file. No luck. My husband sent the file to SanDisk to see if someone there could fix it. Again, no luck. My book was gone. Even though I knew it was gone, I kept looking for it. I scrounged for any printed copies, searched my old computer hard drive that had crashed a few months prior, as well as all possible places on my new computer. It felt like someone intentionally tried to hurt me. I prayed and cried. I looked at what was there and cried some more.

Putting it in perspective, it was a minor setback. I was devastated, but in comparison to what other people were going through, devastation was a strong word. Most of the changes from the past year's work were gone, but it wasn't a total loss.

Still I went through the five stages of grief (look up Elizabeth Kubler-Ross' work on the stages of grief). It was necessary for me to clear the emotion in order to clear my head before I was able to write again. I took a short trip to get away. On the trip, I decided to start where I left off so I could have the feeling I was moving forward. Little by little, I went back to the places that needed fixing and rewriting. While this was happening, my friends tried to help me shift my perspective. "You will make it better," they told me. That was the last thing I wanted to hear, but they were right. It is better.

This experience is a great example of persevering. You get hurt, clear the emotion, take baby steps, reassess the situation, go back to the place that needs fixing, clear the emotion again, take another step forward, heal, pick yourself back up, and rewrite your happily ever after. There must be a reason this happened, and I may never know it. I didn't let the situation and the emotion of devastation stop me. The book is here and it's for you.

Keep your process in perspective. You are making progress. You may not see how far you've come. You may be too close to the situation to see all perspectives. Here is where a coach or others can shine light. Once in a while, a good friend will offer wonderful feedback. Pay attention to messages that come to you through others.

Shifting your perspective can make all the difference in how you feel and approach a situation. There will be ups and downs. During the downs, allow yourself time to sit and be with yourself. Allow the emotion to pass. Then get up and start moving again. Accomplish one small task you've been meaning to get to and you'll soon feel better.

Celebrate the progress you've made even if it seems small. Celebrate something you've accomplished like shifting your thinking or actions. You are making progress while in process. You are reaching something much greater than yourself. You are becoming your best self. You are taking baby steps and some big steps too. Shifting your perspective gives you an opportunity to see things in a different way that can give you strength.

SUMMARY

Persevering is putting forth consistent effort; by doing so, you develop and strengthen your courage. The key to perseverance is consistency. When you apply courage, commitment, resilience, self-care, and perspective repeatedly, you take care of yourself to allow your best self to shine.

Challenge yourself to choose differently for your life. This requires thinking and acting differently. Step away from fear and into action, even if you don't know where your steps will lead. Remember, fear is the result of a *perceived* threat. Focus on what you want more. Take baby steps and keep stepping.

Commit to showing up, regardless of how you feel. When you show up, things will shift. Understand your reason behind your commitment. *You are worth it.* You have a reason for taking this journey, and it is much larger than yourself. Think big picture. The reason is what makes your heart beat again.

Most importantly, take care of yourself during this process. Be gentle with yourself. Say to yourself kind words of affirmation and surround yourself with positive people. Find joy in every day. When you get stressed out, stick to your healthy lifestyle. When you get knocked down, pick yourself up and hit the reset button. Take time for you and enjoy your individual self.

An open mind allows for growth and brings in opportunities. Be willing to shift perspectives. A closed mind stagnates and shuts out opportunities. It offers only one perspective and it limits what is possible.

Your bag is packed with powerful, positive tools. You have everything you need to take the next step. Answer the following recovery questions and you will begin your recovery. In the next chapter, Releasing Guilt with Forgiveness, you will begin to clear the emotions that are getting in your way. Get ready to open your heart once more.

RECOVERY EXERCISE

Write about a time when you were courageous. What happened? How did you feel?

_____
_____
_____
_____
_____
_____
_____
_____
_____
_____
_____
_____
_____
_____
_____
_____
_____
_____
_____
_____
_____
_____
_____
_____
_____
_____
_____

Where in your life do you wish to demonstrate more courage?

_____

_____

_____

_____

_____

_____

_____

_____

_____

_____

_____

_____

_____

What keeps you from moving forward?

_____

_____

_____

_____

_____

_____

_____

_____

_____

_____

_____

_____

_____

_____

What perspective or story needs to shift for you to move forward?

_____
_____
_____
_____
_____
_____
_____
_____
_____
_____
_____
_____
_____
_____

With regard to your answer to the last question above, what is a new perspective or new angle you can take?

_____
_____
_____
_____
_____
_____
_____
_____
_____
_____
_____
_____
_____
_____
_____

How do you typically respond under stress?

_____

_____

_____

_____

_____

_____

What is one small thing you will do to take care of yourself?

_____

_____

_____

_____

_____

_____

What will keep you on track?

_____

_____

_____

_____

_____

_____

7

RELEASING GUILT WITH FORGIVENESS

"There is no coming to consciousness without pain. People will do anything, no matter how absurd, in order to avoid facing their own Soul. One does not become enlightened by imagining figures of light, but by making the darkness conscious."

—Carl G. Jung

Forgiveness is three-dimensional. There are those you need to forgive, so why not offer up forgiveness to them? There are those you want forgiveness from, so why not petition them for it? And lastly, probably the most important is forgiveness of self.

FEELING GUILT

Is guilt learned? Guilt is an emotion that comes about when you feel you have violated a rule, a person, or a moral. Where did this feeling originate? Why is it that some people can do horrible things and seem to show no remorse?

Parents are the best hoarders of guilt. As parents, you blame yourself for all of your children's hurts, poor decisions, and addictions. However, your children are given free will as you were given. They, too, have the choice of making decisions for their lives. Some of those decisions may not be in their best interest.

Let me offer a new perspective on guilt: Your ego is getting in the way. Your ego holds you back when it allows room for guilt. Most of the time when you feel guilt, you are blaming yourself for things you cannot take credit for; therefore, why should you hold onto guilt? You shouldn't. Then how do you let go of it? The antidote of guilt is forgiveness.

It's wise not to take on other people's offenses. Their battle is not yours. Let them work through their opportunity for growth. Stay neutral, keeping emotion out of it, so you can be the best support available. Taking on other people's offenses does nothing but add fuel to the fire. Nothing good comes of it.

REQUESTING FORGIVENESS

When you request forgiveness, you are freeing yourself from the guilt, shame, and overall conflict. You say your piece so you can have your peace. You are offering an opportunity for healing to occur. The request for forgiveness requires a shift in your heart as well as the person who was hurt.

Requesting forgiveness brings you to a place of humility. There is nothing wrong with humility. It is a requirement for great leaders. Take a look at what role you played and hold yourself accountable. Each person plays a role in drama.

When there is conflict between two people, it usually has a ripple effect on others. Think about your work group and how one conflict impacts the whole team. Everyone is having conversations behind closed doors and spreading division. The same thing happens in families. Making a request for forgiveness is an opportunity to make amends for the greater good, not only for yourself. If the other person does not forgive you, at least the burden now lies on him or her. You no longer need to be consumed by the emotion or circumstances. You let go. You did what you could and you tried. Your heart is clean.

Once you've requested forgiveness, you are *almost* free, except you still need to forgive yourself.

Forgiving Yourself

People get angry with one another when one of their core values has been violated. Same thing is true for you. When you violate your own core values, you get mad at yourself. When you violate someone else's, you probably violate yours too. The values between two people could be different from one another; however, the violation is still there.

Think of a decision you made that you now regret. Forgive yourself. Think of a time when you lost self-control. Forgive yourself. Think of a time when you rebelled against your parents or spouse. Forgive yourself. Think of a time when you were self-destructive. Forgive yourself. The point is there are many opportunities to forgive yourself. Remember, everyone has a role he or she has played. It isn't all on you. Everyone has choices and free will—and no one is perfect. You have permission to forgive yourself. It's okay. Really.

Giving Forgiveness

Put yourself in the other person's shoes. When was a time when you hurt someone else? How did you feel? This was a turning point in your relationship. You felt like crap inside. You wanted everything to go back to the way it used to be. You wanted a free "get out of jail" card. You wanted your mistake to be pardoned. Empathy for the other person is key to forgiving someone who hurt you.

Ego, once again, gets in the way of offering forgiveness to someone else. Here you find yourself in the role of persecutor.

You think you're better than the other person. You aren't. Get over yourself. You are as guilty as the next person. Stop pointing fingers and look at your own words, responses, behaviors. Humility goes a long way.

Emotion gets in the way of giving forgiveness. You hold onto anger as if it's a good thing. You feel powerful as if you have some control. The reality is the only thing you have control over is yourself—your thoughts, emotions, behaviors. You aren't your best self when you are angry. This anger brings fuel to the fire, which could bring more consequences. Work through your emotion.

When were you not at your best? When did you do something wrong? When did you need forgiveness from someone else? Didn't you wish the other person could see and hear your perspective of the situation? Didn't you want your relationship to be on better than good terms?

No one is perfect. Give forgiveness and receive forgiveness. The law of reciprocity—give and you shall receive. Treat others as you wish to be treated. Seems simple. At times, I know it isn't. Think on a higher level. Think on a spiritual level.

STORY OF FORGIVENESS

For years, my abortion stuck with me like a disease eating away at me. I asked God to forgive me of my sin. Eventually, I knew He had forgiven me. I still felt the yucky pain inside and didn't understand why. Then I had an aha moment. I couldn't help others with their pain until I resolved the pain within me! I needed to forgive myself. It was as if the burden were instantly removed in that moment. I realized there was something greater than me, something greater than my past circumstances, and my response to the situation. To continue

> TO CONTINUE TO HOLD ONTO THE GUILT, WHICH WAS STOPPING ME FROM HELPING OTHERS, WOULD BE SELFISH.

to hold onto the guilt, which was stopping me from helping others, would be selfish. I found something of greater value than holding onto the shame and guilt. I surrender the shame and guilt to be of service to others.

> *"Forgiveness is the key to action and freedom."*
> —Arendt Hannah

I value life as precious and not to be wasted. The abortion went against that core belief. Here is where depression creeps in. Depression is anger turned inward toward self. This is why forgiveness of self is necessary not only to be able to function but to become whole again.

Forgiveness is for me in all of my victim states. I refuse to be a victim. Forgiveness is the key to moving you out of being a victim. I forgive myself for the decision because I need to heal and help others. I forgive every person who made me feel pressured to go forward with the abortion.

I seek to live in alignment with my core value of freedom. If I am holding on to shame and guilt, I am not free. If I am carrying around bitterness, anger, or grudges, then I am unable to let go of the pain. I was stuck in my emotion and pain, unable to get past the traumatic event and its consequences. I've reached a point of healing where I can now talk about it with others. It only took me twenty-six years!

> *"Depression is nourished by a lifetime of un-grieved and unforgiven hurts."*
> —Penelope Sweet

FORGIVENESS IN RECOVERY

You can see how my story of forgiveness is three-dimensional. I asked God for forgiveness and I received it. I then realized I needed to forgive myself and received it again. It's a

RELEASING GUILT WITH FORGIVENESS

three-dimensional perspective: Give forgiveness. Ask for forgiveness. Receive forgiveness. Working on forgiveness in this
three-dimensional perspective increases restoration of self.

If I want forgiveness from others, I must give it back freely
to others. I am not a victim. I consciously choose not to be
a victim. It is not always easy to get through the process. It
takes conscious awareness and desire to get past the emotion,
but it is worth it. You are worth it!

SUMMARY

By now, you see the power in forgiveness and how it benefits
you in moving forward. I hope it will not take you twenty-six
years or even a year to get to the point where you are able to
forgive and move forward. Sometimes, you violate you, and
you need to forgive you. When you are hurt, learn from the
pain, forgive, and move forward.

Have hope knowing that pain ends. When I had my aha
moment, I was sitting in solitude, spending time with myself.
Spend quiet time with yourself and have the intention to work
through this difficult muck. Allow yourself to be vulnerable
and let your tears release the pain. There is hope. There are
better days ahead.

H – Hold

O – On

P – Pain

E – Ends

You will not want to get stuck on the Isle of Muck. This
Isle actually exists! It is located on the west coast of Scotland.
It is very small; two miles long and one mile wide! Imagine
your muck being so small, comparatively speaking, to your
life's mission and purpose. It is only our thoughts and ego that

79

make our muck the size of Mount Everest! Get over yourself and become your best self. Forgiving yourself is in line with loving yourself. In the next chapter, you get all of the love and attention you've ever needed to feel valued.

RECOVERY EXERCISE

The questions and exercises are for you to start forgiving in all three dimensions.

What do you need to forgive yourself for?

_____
_____
_____
_____
_____
_____

Write a letter to yourself. Explain what happened. Tell yourself why it is important for you to forgive yourself.

Dear _____,
      (Your Name)

I forgive you for . . .

_____
_____
_____
_____
_____
_____
_____
_____
_____
_____

RELEASING GUILT WITH FORGIVENESS

Who else do you need to forgive?

Even if this person has passed on, you can still write him or her a letter of forgiveness. Write out what happened and include what you needed from this person. What do you wish this person would have said to you? How did you want to be treated by this person? Include it all in the letter.

Dear _____,

I forgive you for . . .

_____

_____

_____

_____

_____

_____

_____

_____

_____

_____

_____

_____

_____

_____

_____

_____

_____

_____

_____

_____

_____

_____

_____

_____

_____

_____

_____

_____

_____

_____

_____

_____

_____

_____

_____

_____

_____

_____

What was your role in this situation?

_____

_____

_____

_____

_____

_____

_____

_____

_____

_____

_____

_____

What do you wish you would have done differently?

_____
_____
_____
_____
_____
_____
_____
_____
_____
_____
_____
_____
_____

What is something you can do to open the opportunity for communication? Or how will you ask for forgiveness from others (if they are still present)? Remember, this is so you can be free.

_____
_____
_____
_____
_____
_____
_____
_____
_____
_____
_____
_____
_____

8

LOVING YOURSELF

"For fast-acting relief, try slowing down."

—Lily Tomlin

In Chapter 7, you learned forgiveness is one of the most powerful things you can do for your growth. It's an attribute of self-care. By showing forgiveness, you are showing love of self and others. Sometimes, forgiving yourself is the first step you need to take toward loving yourself. The truth is if you don't love yourself, you can't do much to help others or have any hope for a better life, and this chapter shows you how to learn to love and take care of yourself.

SLOWING DOWN

Being "busy" has been viewed as a positive thing. However, it's over-used and over-rated. Being busy inflates your ego and deflates what's most important. Being busy has been attached to meaning you are important. It's often used as an excuse to not do something. Be honest; the majority of the things you are busy with are a waste of time. You aren't as busy as you think you are when you look at how you really spend your time. And it's funny to me when people tell me that I'm busy! Stop making assumptions about others. If you are assuming I'm busy because of something you don't want to do—that's on you. You're making up a story and an excuse.

Social media is one of the biggest time wasters today. This social media craze has created a new addiction. Constantly being "on" is draining your internal batteries, and you need to unplug completely. The working culture of today includes texting, intermittently answering instant messages and emails, in addition to screwing off on social media, all while trying to do some actual work. Self-care looks different from how it did fifty years ago because of technology; there are more distractions. It's no wonder folks are behind schedule. You must unplug from it all!

According to Dr. John Medina, author of *Brain Rules*, when it comes to paying attention, multitasking is a myth. Your brain must shift each time you shift to a different activity. He states, "When you are always online, you are always distracted." He also tells us that people who are interrupted take 50 percent longer to complete a task and make 50 percent more errors. Multitasking and interruptions lead to stress. Stress then spills over into cancer, high blood pressure, and heart attacks; well, you know the list. You are more stressed than you realize. Kind of like going for a massage when you didn't realize your body was hurting until someone touched you.

Your mind is on overload! Do your thoughts start to wander as you sit in a meeting? Are you thinking of all you need to get done or all the other places you'd rather be? This is a good sign you aren't spending enough time with yourself by yourself. Life is overwhelming. Slow down and restructure. Let's take a look at your work life.

BALANCING LIFE

Coming from Human Resources, I'm a bit jaded. The work culture I experienced was not in alignment with who I am at my core. I'm a creative person, so to be put in a box doesn't work for me. My career that I worked so hard for and spent a majority of my life working at ended up becoming a dreaded day job. It served a purpose for a moment of time in my life, however, I realized I wanted something more. It wasn't fulfilling me any longer. I had to get out. Take an inventory of who you are and where you work. Is it providing meaning to your life?

I love my country and I have served in the military. Serving in the military is an honor that supports the greater good—a cause that is bigger than myself. The sacrifice is worth it. America is still a country where freedom rings. Let's keep it that way. Are your work sacrifices worth it?

My point is for you to wake up to the desires of your heart. Stop being the sleeping, walking zombie. If you are living unconsciously and moving

> MY POINT IS FOR YOU TO WAKE UP TO THE DESIRES OF YOUR HEART.

about on autopilot, then reflect and recover your destiny. It is the only way you'll ever reach it! If you'd rather work for yourself, then start taking steps to become an entrepreneur. If you need more flexibility, then find something that will give you flexibility. Breaking News: You don't have to put up with a work environment that isn't feeding your intrinsic values. You also don't need to put up with a shitty boss. You have knowledge, skills, and abilities you can take somewhere else. You are valuable. Loving yourself is recognizing your value.

Work/life balance is a struggle for people who fail to set boundaries. It's up to you to choose a work schedule that gives you the time you need to care for yourself. I never understood why someone would want to spend more time at work, especially working for someone else's dreams. There's a difference between working a job and fulfilling your passion. For some, work is where their passion is found, but for others, I would bet it is a meaningless job. Perhaps your career may have started as a passion and now the wick has fizzled out. If you aren't happy with your work, you might consider making a transition or starting a business. In other words, if what you have going right now isn't working, start dreaming again and take steps toward a new passion.

It kills me to see people working overtime, spending less time with their kids. Imagine working your normal hours at the overtime rate without the overtime hours. If you need the overtime to pay your bills or support your hobbies, you can do better by getting a higher paying job. Stop living beyond your means or working in the wrong position. What would it take for you not to work overtime? Or a second job? What if you had *one* better paying job? Look at your situation and make a change for the better.

Being a workaholic is an issue of the ego. People think they are so important that they need to work more hours. Ego heads think the company cannot survive without them. I told you, I'm a little jaded. I've seen abuse of overtime repeatedly as a lack of integrity (by the employee) and a lack of efficiency (by the company). If you are working more than what's necessary, stop doing it! Seriously, get a life outside of work.

If *you're telling yourself* you *must* have a day job, then ensure you keep it as a "day" job and not an around-the-clock job. Take your breaks and lunches in order to rest your mind and body. You already know you'll be more productive when you take care of yourself. Go home when your shift ends! Your family needs you. If you don't have a family, remember, you need you.

Take your vacation. You aren't impressing anyone but yourself when you stack up your time. There is a reason the company offers this benefit. It isn't there to entice you to take the job. It's like a maintenance plan. You need a break to maintain your wellbeing. If taking time off is frowned upon and is part of the company culture, find a new company. It's that simple. Really. Wearing yourself out to the point of getting sick is not worth the pennies attached.

Sick time is for those times when you or your family member gets sick. I'm not going to spell out a company policy here. If you are the type of person who needs permission to take a sick day, I give you permission! Take a sick day even when you aren't physically sick but need a mental health day. Our minds need breaks too!

Overworking is a clear sign of a lack of self-care. Failure to take care of yourself also ultimately makes you less productive at your job. To all the bosses out there, support healthcare in a new way by supporting your employees' work/life balance. It's going to be cost-effective in the long term. Your employees will feel valued, thus reducing overturn. Happy employees affect the bottom line in a positive way.

To all the parents out there, your family will be as healthy as you. Take the lead and be a role model of self-care. Children need their parents physically present. Model for your children healthy eating, routines, boundaries, and balance. Your kids are watching you, whether you realize it or not. Stop going along with what everyone else is doing. Be your best advocate and a model for your kids.

Restructure your daily routine to allow yourself time to be alone. Be in silence with yourself. Think about the work life you want to create for yourself. Put all of your business ideas down on paper and start exploring your options. In a world full of "busy," what will you do to slow down? You may need to wake up a little earlier, but this sacrifice is worth it. Give yourself the gift of seeing what's possible.

REMEMBERING JOY

Life has a way of catching up to you because when you don't live with intent and don't make changes along the way, you get stuck but time moves forward. You have a family and work, and too often the things you love to do get pushed aside. I used to love dancing alone in my room as a teenager. No one was looking and it was so freeing. Looking back to my childhood, I remembered how I used to imitate Julia Childs and skits from *The Carol Burnett Show*. Imitating my parents also got a great laugh from my family. I realized I had a dream once of being a model. That dream was lost in the muck of life. I remembered how I felt when I was performing and the response from those around me. These memories are what led me to pursue acting. Yes, even this late in life. As long as I'm enjoying myself, not much else matters. I want to show you that it's not too late.

Taking care of yourself includes pursuing your dreams. It's honoring those parts of you that are dying to come out. When you do what you love, your heart beats. You are excited and have a sense of self. It's a wonderful feeling to be alive again. Honor yourself and pursue your dreams. Let the world see you. Let the world become a better place because you're in it. Let the world reap your God-given talents. You are here to share those talents.

BEING YOUR OWN ADVOCATE

In late June of 2011, I received a call from my mom. She informed me that she had been diagnosed with stage 4 lung cancer. Shortly after, I flew out to see her and spent the next three months with her until she passed away on October 1. Twenty years or so prior, she was a smoker. Her life and death taught me a few things:

1) The lifestyle you choose today will affect your tomorrow.

2) Be your own best advocate.

3) Taking medication comes with a risk.

4) Life is too short not to enjoy your talents and pursue your dreams.

There seems to be no shortage of sick people. My mom wasn't exactly young, but since her death, I've lost some friends too. Young people are dying of cancer. Losing my mom and seeing her suffer created a hunger inside me to find a better lifestyle. I started reading about food and figuring out what was really in the food I was putting in my body. There are great documentaries made on this topic. I'm convinced the food industry is a huge contributor to disease. I am a fan of Vani Hari, Food Babe. Check out her website at www.foodbabe.com.

There are no excuses as to why you can't eat healthier. It is a process like anything else. You take baby steps. You educate yourself. You take another step. You apply the knowledge. I've heard plenty of excuses from people who are not ready for change. When you are ready to change, you do. Period.

Realizing the corruption in the food industry and the fact that we are all human experiments when it comes to "practicing" medicine, I decided to stop doing what the majority of people are doing. I educate myself and make an informed decision. Same thing is true for my life at work. When I realized no one had my back or really cared about my career, I decided to take my talents and capitalized on my potential.

Diets don't work for me because I don't work for the diet. Lifestyle changes need to be made simple if they are to be sustained. The more I learn about the food I eat, the more I apply and make changes. It's a process. Knowledge is power when you apply it. What I learn about food motivates me to change my food choices. I prefer if you learn to fish for your own information regarding food. By doing your own research, you take ownership. I've included some resources at the back of the book to get you started. Be aware of the source and explore alternatives. My point: Do your own research and make educated decisions accordingly.

Being your own best advocate means educating yourself and doing what you feel is best for you. This is huge when it comes to medication. My mom was given medication throughout her chemo and radiation treatments. She had a stroke. It was very sad to see her lose the use of her arm and not be able to speak when her time was running out. Know what the medication is and the side effects of it before you take it. I'm not telling you what you don't already know. It's up to *you* to decide whether that risk is worth it. Take into consideration the big picture diagnosis. Remember, it's your body, your choice. Mom wanted to go to Tuscany and Machu Picchu. In hindsight, I wish we would have gone on a trip instead of going to the chemo farm.

Don't wait for a terminal diagnosis to start living. Live your life now and do things that bring you joy. You take care of you.

Developing Self-Worth

The outward displays of loving yourself are those self-care steps that were already mentioned. Getting to know yourself, setting boundaries, and returning to those activities you love all assist in developing your self-worth. The experiences and messages you've taken in over the years have an impact on your self-worth. The internal work you do will build your self-esteem. Forgiving yourself and others clears the heart for coming back to oneself. How you think and feel about yourself is what you battle.

The message that was imprinted on my subconscious was "I am not enough." Low self-esteem played out in my life as a lack of self-worth. When I could not value myself, I failed to value others too. This has followed me around way too long and it's impacted every area of my life. Those mistakes and choices I made early in life are due to this lack of self-worth. I wanted to feel valued enough to be talked to and shown that I mattered to the people I loved most. The reality is painful. I didn't get my emotional needs met as a child and had to heal from this pain. I wasn't loved unconditionally for who I am, regardless of my mistakes. I had to find self-worth within myself because I wasn't going to get it anywhere else.

I've spent a great deal of time making sense of my past—understanding where I came from and how I have responded to my environment. From this place of understanding, I was able to choose and practice a different view of who I am. I was able to redefine and refine who I am. This is a work in progress. My message now is: I am valuable. I am worthy of love. I am loved. I love me. I love others. Remind yourself constantly of these things: You are valuable. You are worthy. You are loved.

I've worked through the internal pain. I came to know myself first and then love myself. The more I got to know myself, the more I came to like myself and love myself. This work is not selfish or egotistical. It is to make you whole to fulfill the greater purpose. I believe all change starts with each individual. A simple starting place for all of your complaints—you!

Consciously Loving

In my youth, I latched on to the proverb, "Early to bed, early to rise, makes a girl healthy, wealthy, and wise." Benjamin Franklin first wrote this proverb, but this is Marilyn Monroe's spin on it. If something is preventing you from sleeping, get it checked out. Pain is an indication that something is not quite right and is demanding your attention. This includes emotional pain. Your worries, hurts, and obstacles will pass. As you look at the internal you, peel away the external situations, pressures, and things that are causing you pain or stress.

Ever heard someone say, "I'll sleep when I'm dead?" The world is a busy place. You want to live life to the fullest. You want to pursue your dreams, and yet you have a job, a family, and still need to find time for yourself. I get it. You want to feel good on the inside. To truly feel good on the inside, the work must be done internally. Your external world affects your internal world and vice-versa. Sleep is critical. You deserve a good night's sleep and you are worth it. You will be more productive when you are well-rested than if you are moving forward with a clouded head due to lack of sleep. This is one example. The point is to live and love consciously.

Love yourself and look out for yourself. Value yourself enough to make changes in areas that need it. Whether it's finances, health, family, or internal emotional healing that you need, you are worth making the changes. When you awaken to yourself, living consciously, you begin to love yourself consciously. It takes conscious love toward self to do that.

Summary

Loving yourself is not selfish. It's not only necessary but a requirement for your wellbeing. Your family members depend on you to take care of them because you are part of them. Without your health, mental health included, there is no *you* and everyone suffers. You are setting the example for your family members to learn to care for themselves. Self-care means taking uninterrupted time for you, getting enough sleep, and choosing a healthy lifestyle. Educate yourself on the food you and your family are eating. This education will change your life. Research options for your specific situation and make an informed decision. You can achieve self-care by focusing on one item at a time. Dave Ramsey teaches people to take control of their money so their money does not control them. Do the same for your life. Take control of your life so your life does not control you.

RECOVERY EXERCISE

What do your daily activities include? Write out what a day in your life looks like here; start from when you wake up to the time your head hits the pillow.

_____

_____

_____

_____

_____

_____

_____

_____

_____

_____

_____

_____

_____

_____

_____

_____

_____

_____

_____

_____

_____

_____

_____

_____

_____

_____

_____

_____

What's missing from your day?

_____
_____
_____
_____
_____
_____

What stops you from including this missing piece to your day?

_____
_____
_____
_____
_____

Sit in silence for ten to twenty minutes or as long as you can stand it. Write your thoughts. Think for a moment of the things you did in your childhood that you really loved to do. How did you feel when you were doing them? List them here:

_____
_____
_____
_____
_____
_____
_____
_____
_____
_____
_____
_____
_____
_____

What value do you see in yourself? What do you like about you?

_____
_____
_____
_____
_____
_____
_____
_____
_____
_____
_____
_____
_____
_____

What will you commit to doing for yourself as an act of loving yourself?

_____
_____
_____
_____
_____

What's one trip you've wanted to take? Or what's one thing you've always wanted to try? Or what's one thing you really enjoyed doing as a kid and want to bring back into your life?

_____
_____
_____
_____
_____

When will you book the trip? When will you try something new? When will you start to bring more joy back into your life? Call a friend right now and tell him or her what you are going to do!

_____
_____
_____
_____
_____
_____

9

WAITING ON GOD

"Patience is not simply the ability to wait—it's how we behave while we're waiting."

—Joyce Meyer

A few times in my life, I have put myself in timeout and waited (not without pleading) for God to move. Before doing much of the internal work to love myself, I realized my behaviors weren't serving me in a positive way. By now, I'm divorced with two boys and living alone, which leads me to the next significant chapter of my life.

One day while driving, a strong urge came over me to stop in the parking lot of a large church. I wasn't attending church and thought it odd that the prompting was really strong. Being an introvert, I wouldn't normally stop in a random place and actually go inside. When I went in, I met a woman in the stairwell. She looked at me, wondering who I was, and said, "Yes? May I help you?" I felt like a completely crazy lady. I didn't know why I was there and blurted out, "Ah, God told me to come here and I'm not sure why." Can you imagine yourself showing up somewhere and saying, "God sent me here?" After those words came out, I felt even crazier! Without blinking, she welcomed me and prayed with me. The woman turned out to be the head pastor's wife.

From that day forward, I started attending church there every Sunday. I remember wearing my red leather pants there one time. I was dressed like I was going to a dance club! What in the world was I thinking? By the way, those hot pants later got torn in the knee when I fell off a curb at a party. That's funny to me now. I was a piece of work and still am, but I'm God's piece of art now.

Finally, I decided to make changes in my life. A conscious decision to take a timeout from dating was exactly what was necessary to stop attracting the same type of man. You know, the flashy type with the smooth talk, fast hands, and sparkly things (cars and jewelry). I decided to surrender to God and told Him, "Lord, I am done. I'm done being the party girl." Oddly enough, my next statement was, "If I have to go to church drunk, I will." In other words, I was going to be in His house no matter what. I was committed to doing things a different way, and that meant changing my behaviors. See, I had to show up and God would work on the rest.

It was time I find my prince. I wanted to settle down and get married. This time I wanted to make sure I got the right guy. I asked God for a "man of God." In other words, a man who loved God that I could trust. I wanted a man who walked the talk. I begged, "Just give me a man of God, please. I'm done with the players." I was at my ultimate point of frustration. The superficial relationships that were going nowhere, wasting my time and energy, were no longer satisfying to me. I shut the door to the last relationship and decided to wait on God to answer.

CREATING CLOSURE

Closure, to me, represents an ending and a new beginning. I like closure! It releases me from thoughts, emotions, and activities—all energy spent. It also creates capacity for me to open myself up to receive something new, whether it be a new person in my life, or new possibilities. You can create closure for yourself. In this particular situation, I created a private ceremony. It was as simple as taking a walk around my apartment grounds with intention. It was my way of saying goodbye to my old life of being an apartment dweller. The apartment was perfect for a season in my life; it provided a safe haven for my kids for five years. Five years seemed like a long time to me.

A nesting feeling came over me, like women experience prior to giving birth. Preparing for a change to occur, I cleaned my apartment and cleared out my closet. I got rid of things that held a memory of this past lifestyle. This was my way of letting go of what I had in order to receive what I wanted. I got rid of clothes I had worn to bars and threw away outfits that had a memory attached to it from dating. I destroyed letters, pictures, and gifts. You can do the same. Make a ceremony out of it! Do something that will help you bring closure to the old, and expect to receive the new.

I now wanted something more for myself and my kids. I wanted a husband I could trust and count on to be there as a role model for my kids. I felt life was slipping by me. I felt old at the age of thirty-four. Perhaps I felt this way because my psychologist (the same one who told me I was abandoned as a kid) said I had a few good years left and I still had time to find someone. In hindsight, I've come to realize no one should put a time frame on finding the right person. Have you seen how other people get consumed in their search for that one "right" person? People get married at all stages in their lives. I give the doctor the benefit of the doubt and chalk his comment up to him trying to motivate me to choose differently for my life.

After my ceremonial walk through the apartment complex and cleansing my space, I felt free and open to receiving my new life. My pastor preached, "You could be sitting next to your husband and not even know it." I looked all around that church and thought to myself, "Oh, hell, no, there is *no one* in here for me." One tall white man stood out because he would stretch his arms all the way up in the air during worship. You couldn't miss him. He was 6'3", and he didn't know how to dress at all. His style consisted of a low budget, mismatched mess. I also saw "players" in church and I could spot one a mile away. Sure enough, you give it enough time, and you'll see him bring in a different woman every month or week for that matter. One tried to get me to suck his you know what in the parking lot! Are you kidding me?

Despite this dude, I continued to go to church and be observant. After a while, the tall man asked me for coffee. He was a single parent of two boys who were around the same ages as my boys. Before long, he started to feel like family. Yes, predictably, we started talking about getting married. Being completely frustrated with my past relationships and nervous about any future relationship, I prayed about whether he was the right one for me. My choices in the past seemed to lead me to the wrong men. I certainly didn't want to rely on my own thoughts and feelings because I didn't want to make another mistake. The Bible's words, "Seek God first and lean not on your own understanding" came to mind. As I was praying, I heard a small quiet voice. The words I received that day were, "Just be with him and you'll be blessed." I would not have thought of that advice myself. I was barely walking with God. What I knew was my way wasn't working so I thought I'd try God's way.

I'm not a "Bible thumper" who tries to cram the Bible and God down other people's throats. In my opinion, such people turn others away from God instead of toward Him. Anyway, I considered that silent voice's message to be a word from God, so I acted based on those words. We were married in 2003 and blended our families. Those eight words have given me strength throughout times of turmoil when our marriage looked like *The Rocky Horror Picture Show*. Those words would come back out of nowhere years later. I continuously surrendered and put my faith in God. I could not argue with Him. I am with the person God has chosen for me. I am blessed! I am very happy that we made it through those difficult times and stuck it out.

Sometimes, you have to sit, pray, and wait on God. Too much of my life has been lived without first consulting

> SOMETIMES, YOU HAVE TO SIT, PRAY, AND WAIT ON GOD.

with God, so I can say I am truly blessed to have the husband God chose for me who reminds me to put God first and listen to Him.

BLENDING FAMILIES

As I write this book, my husband and I have survived fifteen years of marriage. I say, "survived" because, at times, the kids' behaviors came between us. I admit when we got into this marriage, I was like Mama Bear protecting her cubs, and he wasn't far off from Papa Bear with his own cubs. For years prior to our marriage, he played surrogate mom in addition to dad for his children. It's hard enough to blend families especially when the kids are in critical pre-teen years. Now add drug addiction to the equation. All four boys tried drugs. Except they didn't *try* them; they went full speed ahead with hard-core drugs. It first started in adolescence with alcohol and marijuana. Then it progressed to every drug possible, and yes, sadly, heroin and meth. Our "drug drama" story is not far off from those you've already heard.

DRUG DRAMA

It's 3:10 a.m. and I can't sleep. I don't know whether my sons are dead or alive. I pray in the moment for their safety and recovery. I don't know why I woke up in the middle of the night and felt I needed to pray. Then I get a call while I'm at work. "Mom, I need you to pick me up." I said, "Who is this?" I knew it was my son; I didn't know which one. "It's Andre. I was stabbed last night, and I'm at Harbor View. They hit an artery." Everyone in this city knows that Harbor View Hospital is where people are airlifted in life or death situations. This was serious. My son could have died. I was in shock. My heart was heavy as I left work and went to pick him up.

At the hospital, I pulled the nurse aside and told her my son was a drug addict so she would be aware before prescribing any pain medication. I was concerned about the effects if he mixed drugs. She acknowledged the information I gave her, but medication was still prescribed. Once my son was released, he went back to using.

My younger son almost died in a county jail. He was found in fetal position by a correctional officer. I never received a call to inform me he was transported out. I only learned of it when my son shared it with me after he was released.

Situations like these could occur any time, and sometimes I would have never known had it not been for receiving a bill in the mail for an ambulance. Apparently, my son had overdosed and been rushed to the hospital. Wow. And I didn't even get a call. Even crazier, this situation happened on more than one occasion.

Another time I took one of my sons to the walk-in clinic, the nurse tried to draw blood but was unable to due to his collapsed veins. Eventually, I think I became numb to things like this occurring. I knew my sons had seen the posters of sucked-up meth users, and yet they continued to use drugs.

Setting Boundaries

Over the years, I learned to set boundaries. Anyone using drugs was not allowed to live at home. I learned to love my sons from a distance. This was part of learning to love myself too. I struggled with codependency. Learning to pause in the moment and ask myself whether they were capable of doing for themselves helped me recognize when I was being codependent. Codependency is doing for someone who is capable of doing for him- or herself. Any time you find yourself trying to control or manage an addict's behavior, it's codependency. Codependency occurs whether someone is using or not. Addicts get used to people doing things for them so when they get clean, the co-dependent behaviors may continue. Get support for yourself if you are struggling with someone else's addiction.

Surrendering

Realizing you have no power or control over someone's use is the first step to surrendering. I will never forget the day my brother sent me an instant message at work. He told me I needed to let go or it would destroy me. That instant message was a wake-up call for my own wellbeing. I needed to let go. I was self-medicating with alcohol. This was not only caused by my sons' drug use but also the stresses at work. The happy hour, binge drinker would best describe me. Focusing on new dreams helped shift my focus. Letting go doesn't mean that you don't care about or love others. Letting go doesn't mean that you stop praying for them. It means you're going to take care of yourself and be there for them when they are ready to get help. Again, I put myself in timeout and waited for God to deliver them from addiction.

Summary

"Waiting on God" is the title of this chapter. The irony is God was waiting on me the whole time. I had to get to the place of surrender before He could provide me the things I truly desired. I needed to trust in Him. I came to a place in my life where I knew my way wasn't working.

Sometimes, you don't have the answers to your dilemmas, nor do you understand them. It's okay to take time and sit it out. While I was waiting for God to move, I needed to look at my own behavior. The only thing I could control was my own behavior and my response to others' behaviors.

Having God in my life has definitely been a benefit. I cannot imagine my life as a non-believer. I believe in the power of prayer and the power of Almighty God. I believe in miracles and deliverance. I don't have a prescription to make it all better for you. You must find your own path to peace.

My enabling behaviors needed to stop, and I had to start loving myself again. My hope is for you to move forward and go after life. Some doors are not opened and for good reason. You already know what doors you should close. To help in moving forward, you can create your own sense of closure that will allow you to start a new journey.

"Ask and it will be given to you; seek and you will find; knock and the door will be opened to you. For everyone who asks receives; he who seeks finds; and to him who knocks, the door will be opened."
—Matthew 7:7

RECOVERY EXERCISE

Write out what you are looking for in a partner. I challenge you to ask God whom He wants you to have as a partner. What characteristics, values, and beliefs do you want this person to have?

_____
_____
_____
_____
_____
_____
_____
_____
_____
_____

Create a ceremony of closure for yourself. Write out the details here:

_____
_____
_____
_____
_____

What or whom do you need to let go of?

_____
_____
_____
_____
_____

What behaviors do you need to change?

_____
_____
_____
_____
_____
_____

What boundaries will you create?

_____
_____
_____
_____
_____
_____

SUMMARY OF SECTION TWO: RECOVERY

Recovery is an ongoing process and requires a deep work from within. The process includes finding yourself again—redefining and refining. Getting clear on who you are starts with knowing yourself. By understanding where you came from and choosing a different response to your past, you can heal forward. Healing your heart is the art of recovery. A deep work within requires forgiveness in a three-dimensional paradigm. Consistently committing to yourself is perseverance. You will heal. Surrender those things you have no control over. You choose your mindset and behaviors. Changing your thoughts and behaviors is what you will learn in the next section: Redirect.

SECTION THREE

REDIRECT

I WANT TO BE A PERFECT PRINCESS AGAIN.

This princess is awake! She has the strength now to redirect her thoughts and behaviors. She is ready to put her crown back on and take reign over her own life! She is clear on what her crown looks like and the action required to wear it. She will let nothing stand in her way.

Section Three focuses on insights of areas of self-development that have shaped my life. For example, living life with intent and a conscious mind creates the path for accomplishing goals. Learning to shift thoughts and actions to ensure you are getting what you want out of life instead of having it dictated to you by an external world. This section will strike up interest in you to allow you to explore these areas in greater depth on your own. There are questions and exercises for you to spend time with so you get clear on your values and how to live in alignment to those values. What you value is what is important to you. When you know what's important to you, it's easier to live according to your values and pursue your passion. When you know yourself and your passion, you create your own happily ever after.

10

SLEEPING BEAUTY

"The key to success is to focus our conscious mind on the things we desire, not things we fear."

—Brian Tracy

Many things can knock you off your path to accomplishing your goals or dreams. Life gets in the way if you do not live each day with intent, and then your priorities slip through the years. I once had a dream for my life, but I lost focus. Life got in the way—well, you've read my story. Where are you in your dream? It's time to wake up. When you do, I promise you that your surroundings will be vivid with bright colors—a beautiful sight for you to see. Wake yourself up and see your dream come-true.

Aren't you tired of wondering, "How in the world did I end up in this relationship? Why do I keep going in circles, making the same bad choices? What is it that I am really supposed to do because this job can't be all that life has to offer?" Feeling like nothing ever seems to change or go in your

NOTHING CHANGES UNLESS YOU CHANGE.

favor? Do you hear the alarm yet? Wake up! Nothing changes unless you change.

The other morning, I went scrambling down the stairs, thinking I had turned the coffeepot on without water. I thought the pot was burning. Nope. There was water. Everything was okay. How many times have you thought you left on the curling iron or some other appliance? Or you set your keys down and forgot where you put them? You don't remember what you ate the day before or where you spent your money, and you have nothing to show for it. I liken these absent-minded behaviors to tuning out someone when you are supposed to be listening to him. It takes a conscious effort to listen, and it takes a conscious effort to pay attention to yourself and what you are doing. Society has taught us to be on the go the majority of our twenty-four-hour day. However, you learned in Chapter 7 that multi-tasking is a myth.

Now let's take this a step further, beyond multitasking, to really living a life with intent. When do you stop and pay attention to what you really want in life? When you wake up from living in an unconscious state, you start to ask yourself questions. What is my passion? Why am I here? How did I get in this relationship? What do I want for my kids?

After I went to college and climbed the corporate ladder, I realized I was making someone else's dreams come true. Being stuck in the muck, I thought a college education was my only way out. And that's how I ended up in Human Resources. It was the first chance I got to experience financial stability. Many years flew by.

I've tried home-based businesses, but I haven't had any luck in those, and really, you are still working for someone else in them. Unless you are the creator of your own product or service, you are fulfilling someone else's dream. However, you can use your day job as a means to get to your dream. I never qualified for welfare. Thank you, Jesus! That's one less system to become codependent on. At some point, you'll need to become self-sufficient. If I were on welfare today and staying home, I would definitely be honing my business skills and taking baby steps toward starting my own business. This system was never meant to be a permanent fix.

What will it take to wake you up? A tragedy? A terminal illness? By this time, it may be too late. For me, getting up at the crack of dawn (when you are not a morning person) and going to work every day, day after day, to a job you no longer enjoy is hard. When you find what it is that you love to do and get creative in finding ways to make a living at it, getting up becomes easy! You want to get out of bed to do the things you enjoy! When you start living your life in alignment with your values, your choices change and your life changes for the better! The internal fulfillment is *amazing* and your *happiness* is off the charts. You feel as if you are doing *meaningful* work and *making a difference*. You don't have to wait until retirement to start enjoying life.

A coach once asked me, "What if it were easy?" This question stuck with me. Days later, I had a big aha moment. I met with a non-profit organization to open up coaching possibilities with its staff. In my mind, I imagined myself trying to sell my services, then having a follow-up meeting, then paperwork. It felt difficult. What really happened this day was a shift in my perspective that changed my life. I went in, spoke from my heart, made a reference point to what one employee had said, and tied it into coaching. Done! I was offered the opportunity to come to a staff meeting and do group coaching with the staff. That was easy! What if I had listened to the story I made up in my mind? What if the rest of life could be this easy?

When I was working, I'd see the walking dead all around me every day. But now I thought, *What if it were easy to do what I love and make triple what this big, billion-dollar company is willing to pay me?* Some things are easier than others and you will never know unless you try. Granted, not everything is going to be easy. Doing the difficult things grow you. It's all worth it.

Wake up! Start living and stop being on autopilot. How many times have we intended to do something, but failed to take action? When I take action, things happen. Results come!

Summary

Too often, you are living on autopilot. When you are on autopilot, your life slips by you without even realizing it. Then you find yourself turning thirty, forty, forty-five, fifty, and can you believe, sixty? Where did the time go? Wait. You haven't traveled. You didn't get to do your dream job or fulfill your bucket list. Your kids are grown? You wanted to take them to Disney World and expose them to other places. Retire? Oh sorry, you didn't properly prepare and the economy tanked so now you need to keep working another five years. Time's up! You had your chance. Now it's time to say goodbye. What was it you were meaning to do? Regret, regret, regret.

Every single day, you must find ways to live with intent and remain laser-focused on your intentions. Set an intention and take action. This is the only way to get out of the muck!

Nothing changes, until you change. When you take action and expect results, you will manifest your dreams and goals. Expect the things you want to come into your life. Keep your intentions in front of you where you can see them and remain focused on them. Thank God for what is to come as if it has already happened.

How much more time will you let slip by? Wake up Sleeping Beauty and realize you can have your dream life. You need to get clear on what that looks like and take action. Continue to stretch your thinking and go bigger and bigger with your dreams. Put forth the effort and see where it takes you.

REDIRECTING EXERCISE

What are your dreams?

_____

_____

_____

_____

_____

_____

_____

_____

_____

_____

_____

_____

_____

If you had ten years to live and at the end of the ten years, you were still doing what you're doing now, would you be satisfied?

_____

_____

_____

_____

_____

_____

_____

_____

_____

_____

_____

_____

_____

What is your first step in moving toward your dream?

_____
_____
_____
_____
_____
_____

Set an intention, create the action, and *expect* to manifest the outcome.

I intend to _____. The action I will take is _____ by (date) _____, and by doing so, I expect (outcome) _____

11

CHANGING THOUGHTS

"Your beliefs become your thoughts. Your thoughts become your words. Your words become your actions. Your actions become your habits. Your habits become your values. Your values become your destiny."

—Mahatma Gandhi

In his book *A Day in the Life of a Minimalist,* Joshua Fields Millburn created a "16-Step Guide to Creating Your Masterpiece." I like Step #4: Stop Making Excuses. There he talks about how, too often, we "should" all over ourselves. I should do this. I should do that. I should, I should, I should. While "should" can become a pattern for some, I'd like to add a new context to this step: I shit all over myself. "Shit," too, can also become a pattern. For example, I found myself in constant drama. Then I woke up! I recognized that it was drama and I played a role in it. I learned to sit it out, not be a part of it, and not contribute to it. I learned to get away from the people who ignite drama. I no longer shit on myself by allowing toxic people into my circle.

David Emerald's book *The Power of TED** is about *The Empowerment Dynamic (TED*). I love how this book helps you identify the role you are playing in the drama by taking a look at the Karpman Drama Triangle. I urge you to read this book so you can learn to become a Creator in your life and get out of the victim and persecutor roles. Then you will view your relationships in a new way. We have all found ourselves in all of these roles—victim, persecutor, and rescuer—at one time or another, but when you learn to identify them, you then find yourself at a place of choice. You can choose which role you want to adopt as your own. Reading Emerald's book changed my life because it provided awareness that brought me to a place of choice.

Recognize when you are in these different roles and shift to creator. Instead of being the victim of a day job, choose to create your own destiny. This brings me to another resource, the book *Creating Your Own Destiny* by Patrick Snow. Snow provides a well-rounded blueprint for setting goals and creating the life you thought was not achievable. Too often, I see people let go of their dreams and get comfortable living paycheck to paycheck. Life happens and years pass by. Then one day, they realize, "This isn't what I set out to live."

Your beliefs are what you know, and in order to change the ones you have, you must seek new ones. Find people who have what you want, and learn from them. For example, if you want to start learning about wealth creation, seek people who have already gone before you. Learn how they think about wealth and see which of their beliefs you can adopt as your own. Read books about people who have already accomplished what you wish to accomplish. This concept can be applied to anything, and it will put you into action, moving forward toward your goal.

Whatever you want to do, start doing it. If you want to write a book, then start writing it. If you want to fish, then fish. You don't need a boat to fish! If you find joy in something, pursue it! Many people are very creative, yet they let go of that creative side they loved so much. Too often, these things get replaced by a career and family responsibilities. Keep this part of you alive. The joy you find here will trickle into your family and work. Once you decide what you want to accomplish, your support team will surface. The right people at the right time will enter your circle. Start taking action and watch how things shift.

Our beliefs are passed on to us from childhood. For example, what did you learn about money from your parents? Even though I never heard my parents talk about money, I learned a great deal from them. What money-handling patterns did your parents have that you now see yourself repeating? Journal the money story you saw growing up. Regardless of the patterns you learned and implemented, you have the ability to change the way you think about money and break those patterns. Adopt thoughts and habits that move you forward. When you change your mind about something, your actions toward them will also change.

Gremlins

Gremlins are those voices in our head that fill us with doubt and try to bring us down. Richard Carson, author of *Taming Your Gremlin: A Guide to Enjoying Yourself*, defines gremlins as the "narrator in your head." Whether consciously or not, thoughts keep you from loving yourself and hamper you from moving forward. These are the "gremlins" that live in our mind. Remember the movie *Gremlins*? Remember how the first one was cute, until you fed it. The same is true with the negative, dark, and destructive messages these gremlins generously provide to you on a daily basis. When you feed those messages by listening to and believing in them, they become destructive monsters that can take over your life. You must take these messages both seriously and with a dose of laughter. Seriously, they have a negative impact on your health, whether it be emotional, physical, or financial. Although when you face them and know what to do with them, you can begin to find humor and laugh at them. It takes awareness to recognize when it's your gremlin talking. With practice, you will catch on to your gremlin's language. Then the power is yours because you get to choose what you do with your gremlin's words. Think about the negative self-talk that goes on in your mind. These are the messages that hold you back. Do not believe them!

> REMEMBER, YOU DON'T "HAVE TO" DO ANYTHING. YOU CHOOSE EVERYTHING YOU DO.

Self-doubt leaves us paralyzed in fear. The pressure of "have to," may result in resentment and lead you where you really don't want to go. Remember, you don't "have to" do anything. You choose everything you do. The "shoulda, woulda, coulda" syndrome leaves you feeling regretful and stuck in the past. With a gremlin in your head, who needs enemies? You don't need any more messages about not being good enough or not having enough. A gremlin will make you feel like giving up before you even get started.

Replace every negative message with a positive one. Keep repeating the positive and believe it. Take every thought captive and change it. Here are some examples of positive messages:

- I am loved.
- I am valued.
- I am more than good enough.
- I am intelligent. I reach all of my goals.
- I make money doing what I love.
- My marriage works.

The more you practice, the better you get at changing your thoughts until you eventually believe these statements.

Thoughts get in the way of letting in what is bigger and better for your life. When you change your thoughts, you change your life. Remember, there is greatness in you.

AFFIRMATIONS

Affirmations are the antidote to negative thoughts. Affirmations are those statements you make to yourself, about yourself, for yourself. These statements are ones you find power in and say on a daily basis. They are your vision for you. When you say them on a daily basis, you begin to believe them, and then they become your reality. The way you create an affirmation is to write a statement as if it is already true. Do not say, for example, "I am going to be wealthy." Instead, say it as if it is true now: "I am wealthy." More examples:

- I am at peace with my surroundings every day.
- I am confident and courageous.
- I see beauty and abundance all around me.

Make your affirmations powerful and make them yours. Let them resonate deep in your heart. Affirmations are an element of the power of positive thinking.

What profession are you striving for? I am an author, speaker, and coach. Once I understood that being all those things was what I wanted, I wrote them down, looked at them, and started taking baby steps leading up to where I am today—an author, speaker, and coach. If I can do this, you can, too. Where there is a will, there is a way. My life has completely changed! Two years ago, I had a vision of working for myself. I invested in myself, believed in myself, and took a huge leap of faith. There were times of doubt, but I continued to persevere through prayer and faith.

You have a choice; do nothing and get nothing, or do

something and get something. Which would you rather have? You can choose to stay where you are today, and in five years, look back and be in the same exact place you are today, or you can start taking action today, and then in five years, look back and see how far you've come! Five years flies by, so you must take *action* now to *move* forward, even if that action is changing your thoughts. Start somewhere—anywhere!

Invest in yourself because you are worth it. Hire the right people to get you to your next step. I didn't wait for a boss or company to develop me. I took ownership over my own development. The excuse that you can't afford it is your victim way of thinking. Instead, ask yourself, "How can I afford this?" And then find a way to do that! Reading self-improvement books was where I started, along with going to counseling. Neither takes a lot of money. Redirect those thoughts into positive ones and tell yourself you have the money and you are worth it. You are able to afford what's important to you. A poverty mentality keeps you stuck in the muck.

When I decided to go back to college, I also decided I didn't want to incur the debt. My undergraduate degree was paid for by the GI Bill through the military. I heard horror stories of college debt and wanted to avoid it. Once I put myself in the mindset of finding a way, the way showed up. I was informed of a company, ten minutes from my home, that paid for college. I specifically targeted this company to be my next employer. The company paid for my master's degree. In exchange, I worked for the company for two years upon graduation. Telling yourself, "I can't afford it" is you not valuing yourself.

Practice building up the people around you with positive messages. Some people have a natural ability to encourage others. For others, this takes a conscious effort. If you have children, how are you developing the gremlin inside of them?

SUMMARY

In this chapter, you learned you must redirect your thoughts to shift behaviors to move forward in life. Seek people and information that have what you want so you can start shifting how you think. Once you change your thinking, you change your life.

You must become aware of the negative thoughts and change them to positive ones. Positive thoughts eventually become positive beliefs. Affirmations are the antidote for your negative thoughts. Be confident in what you are telling yourself and believe it! Stop being in drama, whether it is your own or someone else's. Recognize the roles you are allowing yourself to play. Start focusing on the life you want to create and take action.

REDIRECTING THOUGHTS

Create affirmations for yourself: Start with a negative thought you hear and turn it into a positive one.

_____

_____

_____

_____

_____

_____

Important

Place it where you can see it *daily*. Repeat it over and over until it sinks into your *heart*. Keep this affirmation until you believe it and then move on to the next one. Continuously build yourself up.

Redirecting Behavior

What three actions will you take to start creating the job, relationship, or life you desire?

1. _____
   _____

2. _____
   _____

3. _____
   _____

What messages will you start to speak to your kids to build them up?

_____
_____
_____
_____
_____
_____

12

KNOWING YOUR VALUES

"Maturity is achieved when a person postpones immediate pleasures for long-term values."

—Joshua L. Liebman

Have you ever really taken the time to think about what your values are? Seriously considering a word that represents what you value is essential to creating a solid foundation. Knowing your values and living in alignment with those values is priceless.

See what your top three to five are for you—not for your parents, society, or anyone else, but for you. You may have adopted some values and not even realized it. You might have taken on some values from your parents, church, friends, or society. You may have changed some values based on experiences. Your values can certainly shift throughout your life as you continue to grow and develop. What you valued yesterday may not be what you value today.

Take a moment to examine the following list of values. Many other values exist beyond what is listed here. The ultimate goal is to have one set of values to live your life in alignment with your core being. Add your value if it is not listed here. Circle your top five values:

Achievement	Influence
Advancement	Inner Harmony
Adventure	Intelligence
Affluence	Integrity
Authority	Intimacy
Balance	Kindness
Beauty	Knowledge
Belonging	Love
Challenge	Loyalty
Change	Orderliness
Clarity	Peace
Collaboration	Perseverance
Community	Personal Growth
Competence	Physical Fitness
Competition	Power
Contribution	Recognition
Courage	Relationship
Creativity	Risk
Fame	Security
Family	Solitude
Financial Security	Spirituality
Freedom	Stability
Friendship	Status
Fun	Unconditional Love
Happiness	Vitality
Health	Wealth
Humor	Wisdom

The words listed mean different things to different people. Take each word you've chosen and write down what it means to you. How does this value show up in your life?

Freedom is one of my values. Freedom shows up in many areas of my life mentally, physically, and spiritually. Not suffering from pain is freedom. Being financially responsible and taking ownership over my career is empowering. Being able to choose the work I love doing and not having to ask permission to take time off from work is freedom. When I worked for someone else, I felt like I didn't own my life. I couldn't take time off to care for myself. Now my time is that—my time. Like Dave Ramsey, the money-management expert, says, "You need to be not normal." Most Americans spend more in a day than they make. The point is not to do what everyone else is doing. Through my value of freedom, I choose what is best for me.

Raising Children

What are the values being portrayed in our society through the media? What will you allow in your home? Are the TV shows you and your young children watch in alignment with your values? Is the music you listen to in alignment with your values? Being clear on your values will guide you in knowing what you will accept and not accept.

Without doubt, the values the media blatantly and subliminally broadcasts shape our culture. What is the impact of these values on your children and society as a whole? What values do you want to teach your children?

Conflicting Values

When people have other values than you, it does not mean you judge or condemn them. Knowing your values and those of your coworkers can assist you in getting to know one another so you can work in harmony. For example, when there is conflict in the workplace, more than likely, something is in conflict with the two individuals' personal values. Knowing your values will give you a better understanding of yourself and your responses. For example, has someone pissed you off recently? What value of yours was not honored? Conflicting values clash; however, understanding this aspect of conflict provides a starting place for discussion. Getting to know what others value is an opportunity to connect from a different perspective.

Hypothetically, let's say Beth is abusing company time so Victor becomes upset over her behavior. Victor is upset because he has the value of integrity, and that value was violated in this situation. Observe people in the workplace and in your family. Think about what happens when your values are violated. When situations or others' behaviors go against your values, you may become angry, hurt, or confused. Think about the last conflict you had and what made you angry. Which of your values was violated? The same is true in your marriage. Explore each other's values.

ALIGNMENT TO YOUR LIFE

> KNOWING YOUR VALUES AND LIVING IN ALIGNMENT WITH THOSE VALUES IS PRICELESS.

As you work through your values, you may uncover your passion! When that happens, it is powerful. When you become true to yourself, you can live authentically. In other words, you are real and not a fake. You are the same at work as you are at home or anywhere else. You don't worry about pleasing other people because you have accepted yourself and love yourself. You know where you stand because you know and understand your values.

Personal finance expert Suze Orman talks about values all the time. I love how she ends her show by saying, "People first, then money, then things." If you focus on things first, then you have no money when you really need it for emergencies.

Many times, people lose people over money. What would organizations look like if they prioritized their values? People first, then production, then profit. Better yet, what would happen if our society placed value on God first, then family, then work? We seem to be a society living backwards—work, family, God. No wonder we get nowhere fast. Our family suffers because Mom and Dad are off at work. The family then falls apart. Then we ask, "Where are you, God?"

Prioritize what you value and live in accordance. What are your values? Are you living from the inside out (in alignment with your values and what God wants?) .

SUMMARY

Values are an important part of self-development and living authentically. Taking the time to identify, define, and recognize your values is motivating and brings more meaning to your life. Prioritizing your values will aid you in focusing on what is most important to you. Living in alignment with your values is powerful and brings joy. Values are foundational to the life map you choose to follow. Choose your values and then answer the questions in the exercise below. It is critical to do this work. Remember, you are investing in yourself! You will be better for it as well as a better leader.

People are good at investing in the exterior part of themselves but not so much in the internal. Do you spend more money on your outer appearance than your internal growth? How much do you spend on gym memberships, salon services, clothes? But what's inside your beautifully wrapped self? Your internal gift is as important as taking care of your outer wrapping. Both should be reflective of each other. You want to feel as good inside as you do outside! Invest in yourself by working on your thoughts, values, emotions, and behaviors. The next chapter touches on emotional development. First, answer the following questions.

REDIRECTING EXERCISE

Write down your top five values and explain briefly what they mean to you:

1. _____
   _____

2. _____
   _____

3. _____
   _____

4. _____
   _____

5. _____
   _____

How do these values play out in your life?

_____
_____
_____
_____
_____
_____
_____
_____
_____
_____
_____
_____
_____
_____
_____
_____
_____

Is the work you do in alignment with your values?

_____

_____

_____

_____

_____

_____

What do you need to let go of that is not supportive of your values?

_____

_____

_____

_____

_____

_____

What will you do to have your values show up more?

_____

_____

_____

_____

_____

_____

13

DEVELOPING EMOTIONAL INTELLIGENCE

"If your emotional abilities aren't in hand, if you don't have self-awareness, if you are not able to manage your distressing emotions, if you can't have empathy and have effective relationships, then no matter how smart you are, you are not going to get very far."

—Daniel Goleman

Emotional intelligence is the ability to express and control emotions as well as respond to others' emotions. When you are emotionally out of control, your cognitive ability decreases. You can't think straight. The emotion overtakes you, and to get back on track, you need to take a deep breath, pause, remove the emotion, and then continue.

Two subject matter experts on emotional intelligence are Daniel Goleman and Adele B. Lynn. Daniel Goleman points to self-awareness, managing emotions, empathy, and social skill. He describes emotional intelligence as living with the deepest values, staying motivated through setbacks, showing compassion, and knowing how to deal with conflict. Adele B. Lynn describes people who have high levels of emotional intelligence as being the bridge to get people cooperating with one another. Her model includes self-awareness and self-control, empathy, social expertness, personal influence, and mastery of purpose and vision. Foundationally, one must have awareness of self and self-control of emotions. Mastery of purpose and vision are defined as "authenticity to one's life by living a life based on deeply felt intentions and values." After reading the last chapter, you know your values and can see another reason why they are important.

Emoji Intelligence

Emotional intelligence definitely has a place when it comes to social media. Let's call it "Emoji Intelligence." Social media has become a dumping ground for emotions. Everyone who is on one platform or another is relating to the world through social media. Emoji faces help you respond to someone's social media communication. Your emoji face lets the sender know you saw it and how it made you feel. Did it make you happy, sad, angry? An emoji is another way of communicating, and the same rules apply as if it's spoken word. Be aware of how you're feeling before hitting the send button.

You never know who is looking at your social media accounts. Your posts and responses could cost you an opportunity. Be brief and stay positive. If you want to put all your thoughts and feelings down for a given situation, write a book or start a blog. If your post is too lengthy, people, like myself, will scroll past it. Every social media outlet has a format and purpose. They differ from one another. Use them as a tool and use them wisely.

EMOTIONAL INTELLIGENCE IN THE WORKPLACE

Ever work with someone who couldn't control his or her emotions? I once worked for a boss who slammed his door from time to time. This behavior was strange to see in the workplace, and yet eerily familiar to me. Remember, I lived with an angry father.

Perceptions in the workplace are either for you or against you. Perceptions are what others are thinking about you, and often they flow over into what people start saying about you. Take for example a supervisor who doesn't know how to speak to employees in a professional manner. This is a shot in the foot—self-sabotage. When this happens, the perception is you are a loose cannon. Your leadership abilities are then questioned.

How important is emotional intelligence to you? How important are your career promotions and salary increases? By developing emotional intelligence, you can better determine when to say something and how to say it. You want to communicate clearly to get your needs met and, at the same time, not come off as a jerk. When trying to get into a leadership position, outward, emotionally-charged communication can hold you back from being promoted; it even puts you at risk of losing your job. While frustration might be expressed passionately, when anger is behind it, it blocks you from listening to the other person's point of view. And if you're already in a leadership position, you want to avoid demotions or ending up in Human Resources.

Look at those in your organization who have mastered emotional intelligence. How do these people communicate? Often when they have something potentially upsetting or controversial to say, you will hear them throw a pre-cautionary statement out there to soften any blow that is to follow. One director I knew would say, "I'm going to be blunt here for a moment," and then he would continue with what he really wanted to say. The precautionary statement seemed to prepare his audience and make the next statement acceptable. Next time you are in this situation, practice your precautionary statement. Give your audience a warning for what is about to come out of your mouth.

Being a direct communicator can be tricky and could be perceived in an unfavorable way. Being from Chicago and living in the Northwest has created tension for me while working in a corporate work setting. Clashing cultural and communication styles weren't apparent to me until I worked in a corporate setting. Speaking for myself, being from Chicago, I have an edge to my communication. Living in the Northwest, I find people to be a bit more sensitive and easily offended. Your organization's culture may or may not desire straight-forward communication. In my case, I felt people liked this trait about me; however, the company culture didn't seem accepting of it. It became clear to me that my direct, blunt way of communicating is what makes me unique. Coworkers loved me for saying what was on their mind. However, the communication clash with the company culture was a point of frustration for me. I felt like I couldn't be myself in the workplace.

At times, I've modeled having a precautionary statement and it worked. Being aware of how others are perceiving you is important if you want to get a promotion or stay out of drama. The way you communicate can make or break your career. By having this self-awareness, you can self-regulate the emotions behind the words. This is not always easy and takes practice. Giving yourself some time to respond by taking a brisk walk can be helpful. Ask for extra time if you need it.

Staying on top of your personal care regime is an asset to your emotional intelligence. When you are under stress, you may communicate differently from when you aren't stressed. Pay attention to this over the next week to see whether you recognize a difference.

Empathy is a crucial element of emotional intelligence. As a leader, it is essential to understand others' perspectives. To place yourself in someone else's shoes is the best cognitive exercise to demonstrate empathy. You may not have experienced what the person next to you has experienced, but when you place yourself in his or her position, you can begin to understand a little better what it is he or she is going through. Empathy is the bridge to caring and expressing concern for others, which, in turn, creates trust and builds the relationship. Put yourself in your boss' shoes when he or she handles a difficult situation. You may not agree with how your boss handles it, but having empathy may allow you to send some grace his or her way.

> EMPATHY IS THE BRIDGE TO CARING AND EXPRESSING CONCERN FOR OTHERS, WHICH, IN TURN, CREATES TRUST AND BUILDS THE RELATIONSHIP.

Often in organizations, we work in silos and each person has a piece of the puzzle. When you come together collectively and put those pieces together, you are able to see all sides of the issue, and that can lead to a breakthrough. It is beneficial to bring key people together from all levels to problem-solve. Then you can empathize with people in different positions and understand what it is like to perform their duties. Not only does this process allow you to respect your coworkers, but it also helps you see your customers' perspectives.

Another opportunity to show empathy, especially as a leader, is when life events happen to your employee. Events such as divorce, death, or serious illness impact people in various ways, and it's important for you to express empathy in these situations. Showing your employees or coworkers you care about what they are going through will go a long way. When my mother was terminally ill, a few coworkers dropped off some prepared meals while I was at the hospital. My husband was at home when they dropped the food off, and moments before they arrived, he had received the call that my mom had passed away. To this day, I still appreciate what they did. Having comfort food after a long battle of taking care of Mom for months was perfect and well received by family. A plant and card received days later from the organization's leaders was also appreciated. The simple things in life are what mean the most. You never know what it is that will touch someone's heart. Push yourself to show empathy in times like these, even if you are unsure of how it will be received. If employees don't feel like they matter, then the company won't matter to them.

Emotional Intelligence in the Home

"Anybody can become angry—that is easy. But to be angry with the right person and to the right degree and at the right time and for the right purpose, and in the right way— that is not within everybody's power and is not easy."
—Aristotle

Ever notice someone who is angry all the time? Or maybe the person becomes explosive or is known to have short fuse?

The only thing my dad wanted on the TV when he got home was the news. My siblings and I would be watching TV, Dad would pull into the driveway, and my oldest sister would give a warning yell, "Dad's home; hurry up!" We would flip the channel to the news and run upstairs. My dad walked around the house with an angry look on his face. I never figured out the root of his anger, and I was too scared even to think about asking him.

Emotional intelligence, or rather the lack of it, plays out in our homes, too. Being angry at times is normal. How you handle your anger is what's important. When anger crosses over into abuse and has a negative impact on others, the line needs to be drawn. Learning self-awareness and self-control is life changing and empowering.

Families need healing. Instead of putting each other down—as family members have a tendency to do, labeling it as sibling rivalry or claiming it is a way to show "tough love"—let's build the bridge in family to bring out the best. Build your kids up with positive affirmations. Be someone they feel safe talking with instead of them being afraid you will explode. Learn to communicate effectively in a loving manner. Be truthful, bold, and gentle. There is an art to doing all of these at once.

SUMMARY

Emotional intelligence is the ability to express and control emotions as well as respond to others' emotions. It includes the ability to empathize with others. Genuinely caring about others and asking them about themselves instead of always focusing on ourselves is demonstrating emotional intelligence. When you care about each other and have empathy for one another, you create a relationship and a bond that allows you to be productive in the workplace and at home.

Rules of communication apply to social media. Self-awareness and self-control are also necessary when it comes to emoting on social media. You never know who is watching you, so stay brief and positive.

Experts are saying emotional intelligence is twice as important as cognitive and technical abilities. Star performers have a high emotional intelligence range, so they are the ones sought out for high positions in a company.

Performance reviews, feedback, work results, and assessments give you clues to whether your communication and emotional intelligence needs work. Once you've identified an area you want to work on, consider working with a coach.

Together you will find ways that work for you. Each person is different, so what works for one person may not work for the next. Improving your communication will improve your relationships.

REDIRECTING EXERCISE

On a scale of 1 to 10, with 1 meaning you need to work on it the most and 10 meaning you have it mastered, rate yourself on each of the following emotional intelligence elements:

_____ Self-Awareness

_____ Self-Control

_____ Empathy

_____ Social skills expertise

_____ Personal influence to inspire

_____ Mastery of purpose and vision

Now pick the three items above where you scored the lowest and write them below along with an action for each one that you will take to improve this element. For example, if you need to work on self-control, you might write next to it: I will take a walk or call a friend to vent until my anger surpasses me and I will not respond until I am able to face the situation or person in a calm manner.

1. _____
_____
_____
_____
_____

MUCK OFF

2. _____
   _____
   _____
   _____
   _____

3. _____
   _____
   _____
   _____
   _____

14

REDIRECTING BEHAVIORS

"Determination, patience, and courage are the only things needed to improve any situation."

—Author Unknown

Improving emotional intelligence requires a change in behavior—your behavior. When you change your behavior, you not only have a better chance of getting your needs met but also helping those around you. By becoming a better you, you have a ripple effect on your environment, the people around you, and your family. Changing behavior normally comes because you want something or you lost something. Maybe it's a promotion you wanted or maybe you lost your health and that is why you seek change. In either case, you want to change more than you want to stay where you are.

RELATIONSHIP TO BEHAVIORS

Deciding to change means you are willing to give up what you currently have to get what you truly desire. You are redirecting a behavior to your past. The person you are today is not who you will be tomorrow. The behaviors of your "old self" are those that have kept you stuck. You may struggle with anything from being unorganized, codependent, drinking, smoking, using drugs, eating unhealthy foods, overeating, spending or hoarding money; basically, any behavior that you want to change. You are deciding to let the current you go so you can become a new version of you.

THE BEHAVIORS OF YOUR "OLD SELF" ARE THOSE THAT HAVE KEPT YOU STUCK.

Attached to behaviors is a relationship with that behavior. The relationship you have with a specific behavior is something to consider if you are going to change it. There is obviously a mindset and a story connected with each behavior.

I've struggled with drinking all my life. It's a coping mechanism I learned from my parents. Under stress, I liked to turn to drinking. Celebrating, I liked to find cheer in a bottle. It didn't matter whether it was a celebration or a crappy life experience, alcohol was there. Everything became a trigger for using it. Sunshine was a trigger! Who doesn't like to sit under an umbrella and have a lemon drop? Alcohol was a huge part of my life. I had to let go of my relationship with alcohol. It was so ingrained in my upbringing that it was like another family member. I tried to manage my drinking by limiting it to Fridays and Saturdays, as well as the number of drinks. I was the happy hour, binge drinker. If I slipped past two drinks, I wasn't stopping. And the hangovers started to get worse and last longer in duration.

Finding new ways to cope with stress and celebrate are two things that will help, if you are like me. My desire to accomplish some lofty goals required more discipline and focus.

VALUING SOMETHING GREATER

I valued my dreams more than drinking and truly believed I could accomplish them. Changing behavior is one of the most difficult things I've recognized. There is no shortage of people seeking help to combat addiction. The behaviors you choose today impact your tomorrow. If you choose to eat unhealthy foods, you will have the consequences that go along with this behavior. To create permanent change, I believe you must find something you value more than the results of current behavior.

Sometimes you change by default. This means you wanted to change and tried to change but then something happened that forced you to change. Take for example a health issue. Your body starts to speak to you, warning you that you no longer can handle the alcohol, drug, or food. Ideally, it would be great to change before a health issue creeps up or a court of law mandates you change. Sometimes, these situations provide only a temporary reprieve. You can use the default as a tool to stick with the change. A prime example is someone in jail who stays clean and sober, then gets released and chooses to go back to the same behavior. Learn to recognize these opportunities and take advantage of them. Learn the lesson and use it as a tool to move forward in your life.

How are your values lining up with your behavior? How is your behavior impacting your goals? Now look at your behaviors and see how they are impacting your environment, relationships, and family. How are your behaviors demonstrating self-love?

Seasons of Change

I could share many stories about my drinking. There were seasons of not drinking. One season lasted five years. You can continue to destroy yourself with vices or you can decide which incident is going to be your bottom. What will it take to change? How much more pain will you allow? You will forget your last bad experience until you decide it was bad enough not to forget it. You can use your last bad experience as an anchor to change. Remember the bad experience to create better memories.

Seasons come and go and that's the beauty of change. If you are stuck in one season you can change it. If you fall back to old behavior, you can hit the reset button and try again.

Permanent Change

When was the last time you experienced permanent change? The yo-yo diet doesn't count. Relapse is like a yo-yo diet. Before making a decision to change, you must be *willing* to change. Once you are willing, take action toward the change. Your willingness will increase and become a burning desire.

Once your mind has been made up, take the next steps:

1) Take an action toward change.

2) Get to the root of the behavior.

3) Rewrite the story attached to the behavior.

4) Find something of greater value than your vice.

5) Create new habits.

6) Set boundaries.

As I've stated before, all change starts with a decision. Along with the decision, it takes determination, patience, and courage. When you get to the breaking point of wanting the change more than you want what you presently have, you'll be willing to let go.

Changing behavior, in general, requires conscious awareness of what you are doing. You can get stuck in your patterns because they become habits. Your coping mechanisms become habit. If you've always turned to smoking, drugging, drinking, or eating as a coping mechanism, the way you cope needs to change. Until you get to the root cause of what you are coping with, the behavior will be difficult to change. In other words, until you resolve the underlying hurt, the associated behavior attached to the pain will continue to show up repeatedly.

All of the steps I've listed above require focus. Where you put your focus, is where you will find your results. Focus on the outcome. Focus on what your life looks like after the change, even before the change has occurred. Here's an example in the simplest form: I want to lose weight. I need to focus on the results I desire and not food. Focusing on the food is what caused me to gain weight. My point is to focus on the end result.

FOCUSING ON THE FUTURE

Life is precious and I don't want to waste another day on a hangover. I want all of my days to be full of health and life. I've come to know that having a purpose and vision aren't enough to stop people from destroying themselves. Finding purpose will help to bring meaning into your existence. It isn't the end all to be all. You must do your own soul searching to find what is important enough for you to make the change. Once you change your mind about something, you can change the way you feel about it. Once you change the way you feel about it, your actions will also change.

Facing your dreams of what you truly want in life requires behavior modification. The way you currently think and act will not get you to your destiny. If you didn't need to change, you'd already have reached your destiny. Pursuing and accomplishing my dreams is worth more than the next happy hour.

Find a benefit in the change you are seeking. Is your marriage worth changing a few things within yourself? Is giving up your vice worth saving years of your life? Are your behaviors what you would want your kids to adopt as their own?

Think about your values in relation to any and all behavior changes you want to make. Making value-based changes requires a higher level of thinking so they may not come easily. It took me a while before I had my "aha" moment where I truly understood my value of freedom and how it relates to all areas of my life. My values are guiding principles for making sacrifices; they provide me with focus and enthusiasm for achieving my goals. When you live according to your values, you'll have a frame of reference that will serve like a roadmap for you to get to your desired destination without making any wrong turns.

CREATING NEW HABITS

Redirecting behaviors is about letting the old behaviors go and replacing them with new ones. Behaviors are learned, so by redirecting them, you are replacing the old habits with new ones. By creating new habits, you will be able to let the old ones go. This takes work. Think about the behavior you learned and get to the root of it. For example, not picking up after yourself may mean you didn't learn boundaries. Now you must teach yourself and create new habits.

Is there a new habit you want to create for yourself, but you never took the time to focus on it? For years I wanted to take my makeup off at night, but I never focused on it. Some of you may think that sounds gross, but others of you may have struggled with this situation also. I never gave it the attention or time to create a habit around doing it. As I got older, skin care became more important to me. To make this change, I created a fun challenge for myself. Let me show you how below.

SEVEN STEPS TO CREATING YOUR OWN CHALLENGE

Step 1: Make It Easy: Choose one habit or activity you want to incorporate into your life. Be specific. For example, if you want to drink more water, figure out how much water intake is appropriate for your weight. If you want to lose weight, figure out how much weight is reasonable to lose each week.

Step 2: Have Fun with It: Give your challenge a funny name. Mine was titled, "Thirty-Day Rise from the Dead, Total Makeover Challenge."

Post your journey on Facebook, or Tweet about it and pretend you have a million followers. When you know people are watching you and cheering you on, it creates a great sense of accountability.

Step 3: Track Results: Take out a sheet of paper and number it 1 through 30. Then start with the number that correlates with the current day of the month. For example, if today is the 15th of the month, you will start with number 15. Use this sheet of paper as your check-off sheet to track your progress. Keep it where you will see it and put it in a place that makes sense. In this particular challenge, I placed it by my bed.

Step 4: Have an Action Plan: Get any supplies necessary for your challenge. Know what time of day you will do your action. Check off your item every day after you've done it. If you miss a day, pick up where you left off the following day. Hit the reset button immediately if you fall off track. How will you feel at the end of the challenge?

Step 5: Create a Sense of Urgency: Get started now! Begin your activity and do it for thirty days. There is no excuse to wait to get started. Start where you are now. You don't have to wait for the 1st of the month to arrive to begin!

If need be, remove other activities that are less important that would interfere with your accomplishing your goal.

Step 6: Attach Your Value: Know which value you are honoring by doing this challenge. When you honor your values and are actually aware of what they mean to you, it is intrinsically motivating.

Step 7: Celebrate Your Successes: Celebrate your progress once a week or wait until the end of your challenge. For me, it was important to celebrate midway and then again at the end. Your reward should be in alignment with your goal. If you were trying to lose weight, you wouldn't take yourself to an all-you-can-eat ice cream bar. For me, it was a facial at a spa—something I had never experienced. It can be something as simple as buying flowers for yourself! Let the size of the celebration also be in alignment with the size of the goal. A really huge accomplishment warrants something huge in return. Treat yourself and celebrate you!

Lessons Learned

One lesson I learned from my "total makeover challenge" was that "total" is too much to tackle at once. The item most important to me was the one I focused on, and by focusing on it; I succeeded in creating a new habit. Where you focus is where you will have your results! I've been taking off my makeup now for several years.

Whenever you fall off track, hit the reset button. Get back on track. Pick the next day to start again. You may need to do this often. You will get tired of having to restart and, eventually, you will stay on track. Make any necessary changes along the way if something isn't working for you. Your new habit needs to be sustainable, easy, and complementary to your internal work.

Setting Boundaries

Let's get real here. The people you currently surround yourself with are not the people helping to take you to a higher level.

You must seek out a new network of people who have accomplished what you want in your life. Create a support system that works for you. There may be events, family gatherings, or celebrations where you know you may be vulnerable. If you are honest with yourself, you know you will have to sit out certain activities and events. Who cares what anyone else thinks? If there are negative people at work or in your family and you want to stay uplifted and positive, change those relationships or choose to be absent from them. It is your life, and your future is at stake. You must take responsibility for it—no one else can do the work for you. Put your "recovery" first and foremost.

Set boundaries and inform people of them on an as-needed basis. It may come down to saying no to having a simple lunch with coworkers. Do not hang out with those who sabotage your efforts. As you shift, the world around you will shift, too. As you grow, you will attract a new breed of friends and relationships. These new relationships can be one of the most joyous aspects of this journey. When you are becoming your ideal self, you begin to attract the right people and your relationships serve you.

Summary

Redirecting your behaviors takes a conscious effort. Many have paved the path before you; look for those people and learn from them. Once you change your mind about something, you can change the way you feel about it. Once you change the way you feel about it, your actions will also change.

Redirecting your behaviors is creating mindsets and habits around the outcome you want. Figure out how you learned the behavior and your relationship to it. Rewrite your story in reference to this behavior. What value are you not honoring when you do or don't do this behavior? Focus on your end result, not the behavior itself. What value is attached to the outcome?

Answer the redirecting questions below and you will know what your future looks like and that you're not going to let anything or anyone get in your way—not even your own self-destructing behaviors.

REDIRECTING EXERCISE

What behavior needs to be redirected?

_____
_____
_____
_____
_____
_____
_____

What do you tell yourself about this behavior?

_____
_____
_____
_____
_____
_____
_____

Where did you learn this behavior and what does it mean to you?

_____
_____
_____
_____
_____
_____
_____

What value is attached to the outcome?

_____
_____
_____
_____
_____

How will changing this behavior impact your life?

_____
_____
_____
_____
_____

What behaviors and thoughts still need redirecting?

_____
_____
_____
_____
_____

What people, groups, and/or activities can you incorporate into your support network?

_____
_____
_____
_____
_____

What will you do to celebrate your success?

_____
_____
_____
_____
_____

Create a Fun Challenge: Use a separate sheet of paper and put it where you can see it as a visual aide. Write out the following:

(Funny) Name of Challenge: _____
_____

Specific Outcome: _____
_____

Attach a Value (from the list of values in Chapter 12) to the Changed Behavior:
_____
_____

Planned Actions to place on my calendar: _____
_____

Check-Off List

1. _____	12. _____	23. _____
2. _____	13. _____	24. _____
3. _____	14. _____	25. _____
4. _____	15. _____	26. _____
5. _____	16. _____	27. _____
6. _____	17. _____	28. _____
7. _____	18. _____	29. _____
8. _____	19. _____	30. _____
9. _____	20. _____	31. _____
10. _____	21. _____	
11. _____	22. _____	

Have fun with it!

15

BECOMING YOUR IDEAL SELF

"If you plan on being anything less than you are capable of being, you will probably be unhappy all the days of your life."

—Abraham Maslow

What does happiness have to do with becoming your ideal self? So often, people say they want to be happy. Seldom, do they really understand what they mean when they say that—instead, they point fingers at all external circumstances and people who cause them stress. Happiness begins with working on yourself from the inside. You want to feel good on a daily basis by being you. You want your life to be one worth living—one that fulfills a purpose greater than yourself. Who do you want to be? How do you want the world around you to perceive you? What do you want to be known for? When your life has come to an end, who will you have touched, and what difference will you have made?

ADMIRING THE GREATS

Start with thinking about those whom you admired as a child. How did they impact you? Growing up, I enjoyed the humor of Carol Burnett and Vicki Lawrence while watching *The Carol Burnett Show*. Laughter does the heart good and makes life fun. From this TV experience, I took with me an appreciation for comedy as well as not taking myself so seriously. My dreams first began with entertaining my parents by mimicking the actors and dancers on the show. I saw myself being those actors. This vision brought me joy.

For style, I loved Jackie Kennedy Onassis' form-fitting, professional look. Not everyone can pull off the Jackie O look. Beyond her style, Jackie had poise and an elegance that radiated from her. My mother did too. My son tells me, "Grandma had swag." She had her own style. You have your own style, so wear it well. Your style goes much deeper than the clothes you wear on the outside. Your internal qualities also show up on your outer garment. Your smile, expressions, and word choice are all part of what you wear daily.

Strong women face adversity in the public eye and demonstrate emotional resilience. Historical examples are Jackie Kennedy Onassis and Coretta Scott King. Regardless of the situation, they displayed emotional intelligence in the thick of public calamity. Their courage and resilience is inspiring. The people you see and watch, whether on TV or in-person, have an impact, directly or indirectly, on you.

Everyone knows Oprah Winfrey. Oprah is someone I admire for her down-to-earth approach and generosity. I loved her episodes where she would give away gifts that she tagged as "some of my favorite things." I can do this now, on a smaller scale. Sometimes starting where you are with what you have is the answer to getting to where you want to be.

Mostly, I admire my mother. She was all of the above and more. She was fun, loving, creative, artistic, generous, poised, an adventurist, and regardless of whether or not she was going through a dark chapter in her life, I wouldn't have known it. She had tact. The intrinsic qualities and external behaviors that she displayed so eloquently with grace and beauty were admirable. There were special moments when her cuteness would make those around her smile and laugh.

Think about the people you admire whether they are still here or not. What is it about these people you admire? What characteristics and qualities do they have? If you could reach into a person you admire and take a cup or two from them and drink it, what would you be pouring into yourself?

Next think about the qualities you already possess. Which ones do you want to see more of? What do you do to display those qualities?

Knowing Yourself

In becoming your authentic ideal self, it's important to know what qualities you possess and to love yourself for them. What do others see in you and admire about you? If you don't know, start asking! What others admire about you are the reasons someone would want to work with you. They're what attract people to you.

The muck has a way of covering up your true self. You get lost in those crappy experiences that take a piece of us. Then one thing piles on to the next thing. Pretty soon you don't know who you are anymore. You've let go of your dreams. You've lost your sense of self. Working through everything I've mentioned previously—low self-esteem, negative records playing in your mind—never measuring up, not being good enough—all of which results in anger, fear, and resentment, all needs to be cleared. Hopefully you've reflected on your experiences, recovered your heart, and replaced the self-sabotaging and defeating behaviors with empowering actions so the real you can come out and play.

There are many assessments you can take to learn more about yourself. Assessments for various areas include: personality, leadership, emotional intelligence, strengths, etc. Taking these give you insight and awareness of your behaviors, perceptions, and motivations, depending upon the assessment. Going to psychotherapy can be beneficial as well, and your counselor may provide some meaningful insight. Insights allow for space to heal wounds. Counseling is for a season. Continue to grow and seek out help. If something does not work for you, then move on. Find something else. The more work you do, the more confidence you will gain. Become aware of the language and behaviors you do not like about yourself and work at changing them. A coach is beneficial in assisting you with developing empowering language, providing another perspective, and keeping you on track.

Gradually, as all of this work is done, you will start to love yourself again.

Here are my steps for becoming your ideal self:

1) Identify your vision of self.

2) Study other people you admire.

3) Study yourself. (Figure out the reasons you behave the way you do.)

4) Reflect, recover, and redirect.

5) Be the you whom you love!

This process isn't easy, but the more work you do internally, the more you will shine externally. Admittedly, at certain times during my life, I hated my behaviors and who I was. I needed to change and developed a vision for my ideal self. I wanted to be someone who made a difference in the world. I wanted to be compassionate, respected, loved, and viewed as intelligent and generous. This is how I came to think about people I admired and the character traits I wanted to instill in myself. Since then,

LEARNING TO SHOW YOURSELF COMPASSION, RESPECT, AND LOVE IS KEY.

I have recognized I have the traits I've admired in others. It was a matter of gaining confidence, building self-esteem, and owning the value I bring to others. Learning to show yourself compassion, respect, and love is key.

RECOVERING FROM SELF

Your intentions are only that until you put action into them. You can intend to be a better person, leader, spouse, or parent; however, everything starts with developing you. You may want a bunch of external things; however, until you change the internal you, the external may not come or it will be really difficult.

Do you have a tendency to become attached to your material possessions—your cars, homes, clothes, collections, jewelry, even a job? You have to be willing to give up what you have in order to get what you want. This process can be difficult, but when you think of what the future holds (your true heart's desires), it puts everything into perspective. None of this is about the material items. It's about a change of heart. Once you change your heart, the material possessions serve a different purpose. People think people want to be wealthy or rich for selfish reasons. Until you start to work toward creating wealth, you have no idea the amount of work it requires. Have you ever tried? My goal in life is not to see how many cars, houses, or things I can acquire, but rather, how many lives I can impact. The materialistic things are a bonus, and their purpose is to get your attention. Then maybe you'll listen. But until then, I see people chasing after things, jobs, other people. For what? Start chasing your dreams and see how things shift. See how you change.

Selling a home was difficult at first. But it no longer served my husband and me. The kids were grown and the layout wasn't working for us. Temporarily renting a place allowed us to sort through items that were no longer used. It put me in a place of opportunity. I wasn't tied to a mortgage anymore, and if I wanted to relocate, I could easily pack up and go. Once you let go of what you have, you are in the proper position to get what you want. Letting go of things and jobs is an external exercise you can do to prepare to let go of yourself. Changing yourself inwardly will impact your world, and it won't feel like you're stuck in a rat race.

Let go of those things in your life that no longer serve a purpose. That includes not only the physical stuff but also the intrinsic stuff. As you discovered in the earlier chapters, people get stuck in life due to a horrific experience, by being unwilling to forgive others or themselves, or by lacking knowledge about whom they truly are. Resentment, unforgiveness, guilt, shame, and pride. Let it all go. You want to smile again, so let it all go. Outgrow yourself. Similar to your clothing, out with the old and in with the new. Let the "old you" go in order to become the person you truly want to be.

When you recover from yourself, you humble yourself and face reality. Start taking actions in the direction you want to go. Emotional healing brings with it the empowerment to change. Once you work through the emotions, you let go of things, people, and addictions that do not serve you. I understand this can be very difficult, but it is worth all the hard work in the end. Growing pains are necessary, and when you embrace them and learn to accept them, you understand you will be better off for them.

WRITING THIS BOOK

As I reflected on this book's chapters, I saw the sins of my life laid out before me. Being raised as a Catholic, the Ten Commandments were drilled into me. Comparing my life to the Ten Commandments, I pretty much violated every one. With each violation, I deviated from being my ideal self.

I didn't literally worship men and alcohol, but these were things I sought out before seeking God. I couldn't live without alcohol, and I had a problem with lust. I was living in sin by abusing my body with alcohol and promiscuity. I was not putting my relationship with God first.

How many things can we put before God? For me, it used to be alcohol, men, and work. As a struggling entrepreneur, I put more faith into New Age tactics (that didn't work) than I did in the power of Jesus Christ. I was chasing after a lot of gurus and knowledge. I didn't need any of it.

In my adolescence, I was rebellious, disobedient, and disrespectful toward my parents. I wasn't holy on any other day, so I'm pretty sure I wasn't holy on the Sabbath day either! Abortion, adultery, coveting, stealing, lying . . . about sums it up. There isn't anything else left. It's not easy admitting the things I have done. To move forward, it was absolutely necessary to forgive myself. Through this analysis, I recognized life does not have to be so messy. Life would have been less painful had I followed the **B**asic **I**nstructions **B**efore **L**eaving **E**arth. My life has been blessed even through the trials and tribulations. It is by the grace of God that I am alive today. If you do nothing at all with the information in this book, at least follow God's basic principles. It is when you stray from them that you find yourself in—you guessed it—the muck!

"The person who has been born into God's family does not make a practice of sinning because now God's life is in him; so he can't keep on sinning, for this new life has been born into him and controls him—he has been born again."
—1 John 3:9

SUMMARY

Happiness comes with becoming your ideal self. You can have all the money and material objects in life and still be miserable. Blaming others for your unhappiness does not bring happiness. Understanding yourself and the reasons you do the things you do facilitates the necessary change for becoming a better you. Get clear on what you want for yourself so you can live a life of purpose and meaning. Shifting thoughts and behaviors to achieve your ideal self includes forgiving others, forgiving yourself, and removing sin from your life. Do you dare to be great? Do you want to do great things? You can become the ideal person you love. Sin gets in the way of loving ourselves and being who you are supposed to be at your core. Happiness comes with transformation of self. Once you are clear on how you want to act and think, you have direction. When you let go of meaningless things and toxic people, you are free to be you. You will know who you are and what you believe. You will live by your values. You will become the you that you've always wanted to be. When you become your ideal self, you feel free, even blissful. You are fearless and create all your heart's desires.

REFLECTING EXERCISE

Write down the names of the people you admire now or have admired in the past.

_____

_____

_____

_____

_____

_____

_____

_____

_____

_____

_____

_____

_____

_____

RECOVERY EXERCISE

What is your vision for your ideal self?

_____
_____
_____
_____
_____
_____
_____
_____
_____
_____
_____
_____
_____

REDIRECTING EXERCISE

What will you let go of so you can have more of yourself back?

_____
_____
_____
_____
_____
_____

REJOICING EXERCISE

What is it about yourself that others love?

_____
_____
_____
_____
_____
_____

What do you like about yourself? How will you use these things now?

_____

_____

_____

_____

_____

_____

_____

_____

_____

_____

_____

_____

_____

SECTION FOUR

REJOICE

I WAS BORN AGAIN A QUEEN AND THEN . . .
LIFE GOT GOOD, REALLY GOOD.

This queen has earned back her crown with hard work. She is ready to own the new life she has created. She is ready to take a leap of faith! She is ready to celebrate, and she knows there is no greater meaning to life than to have a lasting impact by changing a life.

Section Four focuses on owning the you that you've worked so hard on developing. You step into your power when you fully accept yourself. Your light shines with confidence, and at the same time, you aren't afraid to show humility because you are confident about whom you've become. When you live your life from a place of authenticity, others gravitate toward your offerings. You are here for a specific reason at a specific time. A life of fulfilling your passions and being true to who you are is where you find contagious happiness. You ignite people with hope to believe in themselves. You give them strength and courage to dream again and love themselves so one day they can help the next person.

Rejoice in knowing you've done the work! You've put in the time to invest in yourself. Acknowledge yourself for the work and strides you have taken to grow. You are better than you ever realized. It is time to rejoice in knowing who you are and the gifts you have to offer the world. It is time to celebrate and be happy with the life you have always dreamed of . . . your happily ever after.

16

OWNING YOUR POWER

"Your vision will become clear only when you look into your heart."

—Carl Jung

When you realize you have no power, it is then you step into yourself—and that is powerful! When you know yourself and love yourself, you show up in the world ready to give back to it. There is no better feeling than giving to others from a place of authenticity. Be you in your fullness. Stand up and step into the power of being you. Being fully present and serving from your core essence is the best gift you can give to the world.

RESPONDING TO DIFFERENCES

Women are the most beautiful creatures on earth—they're full of love and nurturing by nature. However, being naïve also seems to come with the original packaging. At least, it did for me in my youth. Through heartache, I have learned the lessons of being naïve. For example, the way a woman responds and communicates with a man can excite him to the end of the earth while the woman may be clueless what is even occurring for a man! What she thought was harmless friend-liness, the man may somehow perceive as sexual; somehow, the communication was translated into something more than was intended. Understanding who you are at the core of your being and how to respond appropriately to men is a bonus. Maintaining healthy boundaries is powerful. When you value yourself and are confident in who you are, you stand firm in your values and hold your boundaries.

Being young and clueless, I considered myself a tomboy. I was one of the boys. Therefore, I saw them as my equals. I was naïve indeed. Working around men all my life, I still considered myself to be one of them. However, as a woman in the working world, while I wanted to compete with them, they wanted to conquer me.

During one of my performance reviews, my supervisor told me I had a great smile and I should use it more. I took offense to this statement. I felt degraded and treated as if I were a piece of eye candy. When I shared his remark with another woman at a party, she said, "What he is really telling you is to smile more at him because it makes him feel good." I think she was spot on! I could use smiling to manipulate a situation; however, by doing so, I would not be my authentic self. On the other hand, I opened a fortune cookie that read, "Use your person-ality and charm to get what you want." Be your authentic self and maintain boundaries in the workplace. Of course, I'm not going to walk around with a smile plastered on my face all day!

Projecting Confidence

Confidence and humility are essential ingredients to own-ing your power. You are worthy. You are valued. You are loved. You can achieve great things. Be confident in knowing who you are, and simultaneously, not so egotistical that you sabotage your greatness. Your confidence will shine through when you forgive yourself for the past, embrace your present journey, and understand that

CONFIDENCE AND HUMILITY ARE ESSENTIAL INGREDIENTS TO OWNING YOUR POWER.

you are in charge of your future. You are forever evolving as a person; you are continuously learning and taking in all that your environment has to offer. When you live from a clean heart, knowing and loving yourself, you emit light.

Some people have perceived me to be arrogant. In my opinion, arrogance tends to come from a lack of self-confidence or not having yet discovered yourself at a deep, internal level. Arrogance could also be showing up as a protective measure to guard your heart and not let anyone get close to you. I've also learned that as an introvert, it takes longer for me to warm up to those around me. This can come across as being stuck up, hard to read, quiet, or arrogant to the external world. People may think we don't want to come out to play with them because we are too good for them. This couldn't be further from the truth. It takes us a while to get warmed up to our surroundings. It takes a conscious effort to reach out to others quickly in a social setting. Do you know how you are being perceived by others?

Humility can come in different forms; for example, knowing when to be quiet is a gift. I have witnessed people at work who talk for the sake of hearing themselves or for the sake of letting someone else hear them talk. It is as if these people have something to prove to everyone in the room. In reality, those in the room wish they would shut up so the meeting could progress. People like this may not realize they are doing this and what the impact it has on the team. Perhaps they are seeking validation that was absent when growing up, or they are babbling. Whatever it is, this behavior serves no one. Humility is the essence of servant leadership. Simply doing what you do on a daily basis in service to others will remove your ego. Want to learn humility? Volunteer in your community and don't tell anyone about it. To develop those around you by showing transparency and vulnerability, rather than by trying to assert your own importance, is the highest achievement in owning your power.

ACCEPTING ALL GIFTS

I will never forget a classmate of mine who said I was "just weird enough" for him to come to me for coaching on a certain subject. I took this statement as a compliment that meant he trusted me enough to discuss with me a topic that others might have thought odd. As it turns out, I was able to help him because it was a topic I had already thought about myself. This proves that being ourselves and accepting who we are, weirdness and all, is truly powerful.

At other times, I am playful and silly. Has your mom ever called you a silly goose? The other day, I came across a quote from *Zig Ziglar's Little Book of Big Quotes*: "Most of us would be upset if we were accused of being 'silly.' But the word 'silly' comes from the old English word 'selig,' and its literal definition is 'to be blessed, happy, healthy, and prosperous.' Who wouldn't want to be silly?

The point I am making here is your weirdness, silliness, and whatever other qualities you may have, are gifts to others. Accept who you are in all of your goodness and weirdness. In these gifts of uniqueness, you will find power and a place from which to serve others. Think of a person you connect with; what is it that draws you to that person? Your uniqueness is what draws others to connect with you.

COMFORTABLE WITH UNCOMFORTABLE

Many years ago, a woman prayed for me and spoke words over me about being a mighty woman of God. This happened during my exploratory years of searching for faith and before I had a relationship with God. When she prayed for me, I felt as if being a mighty woman of God was the furthest thing from what I was at the time. Now, I see myself more and more stepping into this leadership role of being a woman of God. Where there was fear, courage has replaced it. In the past, I was so timid and afraid to pray with someone. Now, praying with others has become second nature for me. To become comfortable with praying, I was forced out of my comfort zone by praying out loud with a group of people. It takes getting uncomfortable to get comfortable.

The more you force yourself, as uncomfortable as it may be, to step through the muck with courage, the more confidence you will build. I urge you to be uncomfortable with the specific area you seek to improve in to grow in confidence. A couple of suggestions for those who desire to gain confidence is to join Toastmasters or take improvisation classes. These two will help any professional with speaking and building confidence.

REJOICING THROUGH ADVERSITY

"We also rejoice in our sufferings, because we know that suffering produces perseverance, character, and hope."
—Romans 5:3-4

I ran into many obstacles while writing this book. I've learned to persevere regardless of how much time passes. I suffer from chronic neck issues, so when my neck goes out of alignment, it creates debilitating pain. Despite the nagging neck pain and other major distractions, like my son being stabbed and my other son almost overdosing in a jail cell, or the crashed computer and corrupt file, I was determined to complete this book, and I have remained hopeful that it will bring positive change for many others who suffer or are simply seeking continuous self-improvement. It has taken me longer than anticipated to complete this work—a point of frustration and irritation for me. However, my resilience during this journey through the muck will be worth it in the end. Resilience has yet to disappoint me. It is something I embrace, even if I don't understand it in the moment; I have faith that by being resilient, this book will be finished at the perfect time.

Rejoice in fulfilling your potential by using the gifts you have been given. There is no mistake that your gifts are needed and necessary. I am not always the most tactful person, and I may come off as being arrogant or cocky, but I believe these are also my gifts to wake you up and give you a little "in your face" motivation to get going. Fulfilling your potential and living the life you dreamed has no limitations, and it can be easy (if that's your mindset)—when you are willing to do the work, you will manifest your harvest. I had no idea how to write a book, but when I made the decision to do it and I felt the timing was right, the right people showed up in my circle. Believe in yourself and know that the support will follow. Rejoice in who you are and what you have to offer. You have knowledge, skills, abilities, talents, and dreams to make the world a better place. Only you can bring these to fruition. Only you know what is your passion.

You are powerless because you are human. Tomorrow is not a guarantee. Natural disasters, terrorist attacks, and illness strike at any time. Be thankful for every moment you have here, and make the most of it by making a difference every day. Be the best version of you. When you come into being the person God created you to be, and you know and love yourself, you become powerful by being you. Celebrate You!

SUMMARY

Owning your power is not about power. It's about being the very best version of you and celebrating this new version.

Understanding yourself and developing your self-worth and confidence brings you to a place of accepting yourself and loving yourself for who you are. Feel good about your weirdness because that is what attracts people to you. Force yourself to get uncomfortable because the more you do so, the more confidence you will gain.

Work on the things you need to work on; continuously self-improve, and don't sweat the small stuff. Everyone has a story. I don't know anyone who can say he or she had a perfect upbringing or life. You make mistakes, but you also heal, recover, and move forward. Be kind to yourself. Know yourself and own yourself! You have talents and gifts this world needs desperately. Step out and use them. Rejoice in who you are and show your authentic self to the world. Be inspiring to those around you by standing on solid ground. Make a difference in someone else's life. That is something worth rejoicing over.

Rejoicing Exercise

When obstacles come your way, how will you build your character? What will you do to maintain hope?

_____

_____

_____

_____

_____

_____

What is it about you that you love?

_____

_____

_____

_____

_____

_____

What is it about yourself that others might see as odd or weird that you will accept and rejoice in?

_____

_____

_____

_____

_____

_____

What will you do to celebrate yourself?

_____

_____

_____

_____

_____

_____

17

EMBRACING LEADERSHIP

"The first responsibility of a leader is to define reality. The last is to say thank you. In between, the leader is a servant."

—Max DePree

Have you ever wondered whether you were a leader or questioned your leadership abilities? I've doubted myself and questioned whether I was a leader. This questioning led me to a decision to pursue my degree in organizational leadership to see whether I could consider myself a leader. The word leadership is ubiquitous in organizations. What is this thing, anyway, that is so often referred to as leadership? What does it mean? What does it look like? If you are in a leadership position, you were hired to give life to the vision and deliver the company's mission. On a daily basis, you are empowering others, developing future leaders, and implementing solutions.

Solving Problems

Colin Powell said, "Leadership is solving problems. The day soldiers stop bringing you their problems is the day you have stopped leading them. They have either lost confidence that you can help or they have concluded that you do not care. Either case is a failure of leadership." Have you ever had a leader whom you've given up on? There comes a point when we give up on anticipating any leadership from a person who has disappointed us day after day, due to his or her lack of vision, action, or communication.

When you have an issue that isn't being resolved with your supervisor, what's the next logical step? Go to his or her boss. I once went to my boss' boss, only to see that nothing changed; in fact, instead of improving the situation, our conversation ended up coming back to me through my direct supervisor. I then realized I was engaged in a frivolous battle. I decided I was only making myself look like a complainer rather than a problem solver. In my case, the problem went in one big fat circle and never got resolved. I was the soldier who stopped bringing problems and decided the best thing I could do for me was to find a different position under new leadership or leave the company. You can't change others, but you can take care of yourself.

At work, you *expect* your supervisors, managers, and lead personnel to show you the way and encourage your development so that one day you might take the helm and steer the ship, or at least, you expect they will give you the tools and training to perform your current duties with excellence. People have expectations of all leaders—both inside and outside of organizations, communities, and government. It doesn't go one way—top down. If you are a leader, your employees, followers, or constituents, expect you genuinely to care about them, and that requires getting to know them. It isn't all about business and products. Productivity will suffer if you don't know how to balance this working relationship.

When you know your employees, you will better manage your workforce. By understanding each individual's strengths as well as his or her passions, you can provide meaningful assignments. It's a win-win for you and the employee. This will alleviate problems too. When you place employees on projects they love, problems will be resolved and you'll probably never know they existed.

Checking Your Ego

According to Robert Greenleaf, poor leaders are those who have the need for a power trip or to acquire material possessions. For them, leadership takes a back seat to personal gains, both intrinsic and extrinsic. In my opinion, the power trip is a false intrinsic gain that breeds destruction. Being vindictive is a form of misguided power. There is no room in leadership for you to be a vindictive person. This power is temporary. Whatever you do to "get back" at your employee will backfire. Keep things in perspective. Good leaders learn how to put their egos aside; once they do that, they open themselves to learning about true leadership.

True leadership is letting go of your own agenda to allow others around you to shine. It's no longer about you. It's about those around you and helping them reach for the next level all while serving the organization's mission.

A lack of balance between home and work could be a sign your ego is getting the most of you. Do you delegate appropriately or try to control everything? If you have a tough time delegating, are trying to control, and are failing to take care of yourself, my simple suggestion for you is: get outside help! Oh, is your ego stopping you from getting help too? Come on; leaders aren't perfect. You are not only setting an example for your employees but also for your children.

The core essence of a business, organization, community, or government will eventually crumble if the leadership is not intact. It is the same with you. You eventually crumble to pieces when personal care is not taken to protect and serve who you are at your essence. In Chapter 8, I wrote about the importance of personal care. As a leader, your self-care is more important than ever. You are serving constantly in your role. You are under stress. You are putting out, so you must refill your tank by putting back into yourself. When you are not grounded, balanced, and working on continuous self-improvement, you are at higher risk of bringing muck into your career. When you are under stress, you are vulnerable to doing things and saying things you normally would not do. Being your best self requires taking care of yourself and continuous growth. Remember emotional intelligence?

Your title carries authority. However, because you have a title, does not give you free rein to act a fool or lose control. To whom much is given, much is expected. Self-control and self-awareness are easier when you are in tune with yourself.

Restoring Leaders

When you restore people, you restore leadership capability. One must know him- or herself to be confident in leading others. Leaders who work on themselves excel at embracing leadership. All of your life experiences have influenced you in some way. That influence shows up in your leadership.

By doing the work in this book, you will develop leadership attributes. Training is great for creating awareness that maybe you need some extra help in an area. With a low retention rate, I question the effectiveness of trainings. But once the training is over, how often are leaders actually stepping up to the plate and getting the help they need? Self-development takes work and a roadmap. In my opinion, every leader should have a coach—an unbiased, outside, and confidential partnership for the betterment of leadership.

The consequences of poor leadership are disengaged team members and disgruntled workers. You will find employees who do everything but work. They call in sick more often and abuse their time when they are at work. And managers will do nothing except put on the façade that they are doing something by merely trying to smooth over any disputes or issues. When you have blatant disciplinary issues that occur repeatedly, but management refuses to do anything to fix them, it is a failure on many levels. Leaders hold others accountable as well as themselves.

Under poor leadership, people take the first opportunity to disembark from the ship. High turnover in any department should be as loud a signal of distress as a blaring horn to correct a ship's course. Yet nothing ever seems to happen to these leaders. They may be passed on to the next organization, or they may be ignored and allowed to buy time until retirement. But for many, retirement keeps getting pushed out year after year. How long will these leaders be allowed to collect a paycheck without being held accountable? Is your company *that wealthy* that it can afford to be a welfare system for these deadbeat leaders?

Common poor leadership traits I have seen over the years include lack of emotional intelligence, rare communication (unless they need something), lack of vision for the work unit, and a failure to communicate overall company goals. Such poor leaders are modeling disengagement. I had no idea what my supervisors were working on from day to day. No connection or collaboration existed between them and their team. Needless to say, after exhausting all avenues, I disembarked and started to work for myself.

Millennial Leader

I've coached leaders who fit the millennial age range of twenty-three to thirty-five. Because these leaders were beginning their careers, they understandably lacked experience and some lacked confidence. None of them had served their country, nor did they have children beyond newborns. I was concerned that if given the title of manager, their egos and pride would get in the way. It is imperative for leaders to be thirsty for self-improvement, not power. The people skills necessary to be a good leader include empathy, compassion, humility, and self-awareness. When you lack life experience, you may find it difficult to have empathy for someone.

> IT IS IMPERATIVE FOR LEADERS TO BE THIRSTY FOR SELF-IMPROVEMENT, NOT POWER.

The great thing about millennial leaders is their energy and eagerness to make a difference. However, sometimes the eagerness to succeed gets lost in the daily muck of managing. Innovative and creative ideas flow from these leaders with the belief that they can actually pull off these ideas, despite the company's economic strain or upper management's pessimism. Too often, however, the crusty old thought-patterns of senior management dispel any hope for the future to change. And the pace at which the soon-to-be retired leaders move out has a detrimental impact on the organization. Today's youth do not have the patience to wait to move up in the company. They move on to the next best gig in town. The pace of change in an organization is something to consider. New talent will not stick around if they aren't growing or if problems aren't resolved timely.

THE NEW GREAT LEADER

Great leaders create a sub-community within a work group that will serve the larger community organization as a whole. Great leaders are able to overcome their biases or at least put them aside in order to lead. They suspend judgment and do not hold grudges. They are there to serve their subordinates. I will say it again: Great leaders are there to serve their subordinates! Stephen Covey explains it best in his Foreword to Robert Greenleaf's *Servant Leadership: A Journey into the Nature of Legitimate Power & Greatness*: "the only way you get empowerment is through high-trust cultures and an empowerment philosophy that turns bosses into servants and coaches, and structures and systems into nurturing institutionalized servant processes." There has been an elitist power and control disposition for far too long. Perhaps we can find balance with quid pro quo in serving each other; however, quid pro quo seems very tactical and superficial to me in its attitude: I will do this for you because I know you will do that for me. A true servant's heart gives freely, not expecting anything in return. Being a giver is who the person is at his or her essence. A true servant's only hope is to have made a difference to another.

The term servant in our society has a negative connotation to it. Some may think of a slave, a butler, a maid, or anyone in service to another. Women, too, have been viewed in this subservient role. What's another way to look at the word "servant"? What if it were a term of endearment? What if it meant anyone in service to another who was motivated by love, compassion, and affection? Servants could very well include our mothers, fathers, pastors, doctors, nurses, community leaders, firemen, teachers, chefs—let it be all of us! Let us live each day with the intent to serve each other and be known for our love.

The other term Covey uses, "coach," is used loosely so it can have several meanings. My interpretation of Covey's use of it above is to be a boss who comes from a place of genuine curiosity. A boss who is curious about each of his or her employees will come to know and appreciate those employees. Then, instead of viewing employees as tools to get the job done, employees can be viewed as beautiful, talented, human beings who are valuable to the work family. Professional coaches ask powerful questions, coming from a place of curiosity and intuition, to bring awareness to others for personal growth. Having the skill of coaching as a leader will go a long way.

Can you imagine what the world could look like if we had servant-leaders with positive coaching skills? Robert Greenleaf coined the term, "servant-leader" in his book *Servant Leadership: A Journey into the Nature of Legitimate Power & Greatness.* He defined it as: "The servant-leader is servant first. . . . It begins with the natural feeling that one wants to serve, to serve first. Then conscious choice brings one to aspire to lead."

The military has great servant-leaders, but the leadership style is authoritarian. Where the military succeeds is by instilling a sense of community within our military command. As I know from experience, in the military, the only family people have is the work group at their duty stations. When I was in the military, my colleagues and I genuinely cared for one another. We had each other's backs. Our leaders wanted to see us advance. At times, they even acted like parents toward us younger service members who needed discipline. If I screwed up, my Navy chief would have me come in early the next morning to make the coffee for everyone else. She must have known this would really get to me because I am not a morning person. She knew her people!

Larry Spear's wrote the ten characteristics of a servant leader:

1) Listening

2) Empathy

3) Healing

4) Awareness

5) Persuasion

6) Conceptualization

7) Foresight

8) Stewardship

9) Growth

10) Building Community

While these are all important and contribute to a well-rounded individual, my favorite is healing. My take on this one is that a leader will heal themselves first to be better equipped to help the next person. Listening to *understand* another's point of view and having empathy to understand another's emotions are also essential. Look at the list and see which ones you can develop within yourself.

SUMMARY

Foundationally, the best leaders are those who have a servant's heart. A leader who is able to bring life to the vision and then demonstrate how each person is connected to that vision is necessary in a world where employees fail to realize the meaning in their work. When you, as a leader, put your people first, they will deliver for you. When you get out of your own way, you can do great things in leadership. Ego in leadership is a waste of energy and time. You are to solve problems, not become one. You are to be the model employee, and that means showing up as the best you. You have future leaders in your hands. Take care of them. Actions speak louder than words, and your words must be in alignment with your actions.

Becoming a great leader requires personal development. If you haven't worked through your own muck, you won't be able to lead others effectively. Those who do their internal work excel at embracing leadership. There is no room for vindictive behaviors, holding grudges, or abuse of power. Letting go of your own agenda and serving those around you is true leadership.

REFLECTION QUESTIONS

In what ways are you already a leader?

_____

_____

_____

_____

_____

_____

Where do you need improvement as a leader?

_____

_____

_____

_____

_____

_____

What is your perception of a servant leader?

_____

_____

_____

_____

_____

What can you do to develop future leaders?

_____

_____

_____

_____

_____

_____

_____

_____

_____

_____

_____

_____

_____

_____

18

MAKING A PROFOUND DIFFERENCE

"The purpose of life is to contribute in some way to making things better."

—Robert F. Kennedy

Have you wondered what life is all about—why you are here? When you get caught up in the daily grind, it's easy to forget why you are here. The quote above sums up a moment of enlightenment when I realized the reason for being here is so simple. To make a difference for others by contributing your gifts, talents, and story is the reason you are here. My heart is devoted to helping people make better choices for themselves and their children.

Even what seems to be a small difference may mean the world to someone. Making a difference is as simple as what you say and what you do to show kindness and love. You make a difference by what you say and the actions you take. It may be for a brief moment in someone's life. Even if it is for a moment in time before someone leaves earth, you made that person's life here a little better.

If you are like me, you want to make a profound difference for thousands of people. I want to see lives changed for the better. If that also describes you, what would you enjoy doing that would also make a difference?

STARTING HERE AND NOW

> *"One is not born into the world to do everything*
> *but to do something."*
> —Henry David Thoreau

Having it all figured out is not a requirement to making a difference. My muck left me feeling low and paralyzed with fear. Yet I knew I could still help others. Most importantly, I learned to do something with whatever resources I had at the time to move forward. It's as simple as setting a goal or clearing out junk: physically, mentally, or emotionally. Create a new habit of this and soon you'll be woken to possibilities and opportunities. When you give to others, whether it be your time or money, you feel good. There isn't anything wrong with feeling good about it. Through these actions, you realize *whom* you love to help, and *how* you want to make a difference.

Until you reach your dream, every day is your SEED day; it's your **S**hine **E**vent **E**very **D**ay (SEED). This will help ground you, especially if you are stuck in a "dreaded" day job. Here is something you can say every day as part of your morning routine:

Today is my Shine Event. I am thankful to have this day. I move with ease and grace. I rejoice and keep my eyes on achieving my goals. I water my seeds with love and care. My harvest is clear. I shine my light and make a difference.

Create your own Shine Event Affirmation to make it

powerfully yours. Starting a gratitude journal is the best thing you can do for an attitude adjustment. Becoming more aware of what you have and being truly thankful adds perspective. You start to appreciate the smallest moments and things in life, which causes a shift inside you.

You don't have to get another degree or more money to be valued. You do need thoughts and behaviors in alignment with what you want to achieve. When you are stuck in an area, it can hold you back—for years! Get help to move your dreams from imagination to existence. Start now with the resources you have and don't look back. Keep your motives in check. Know why you do the things you do.

BEING TRUTHFUL ABOUT MOTIVES

A TED Talk by Dan Pink speaks about how the carrot and stick theory of motivation is ineffective and old school. He breaks it down into three things that motivate: autonomy, mastery, and purpose. I agree with his research. Autonomy speaks freedom to me—again one of my values. To become a master at anything is a challenge, and the challenge of it all is what I find motivates me. Understanding what motivates you is another key to knowing yourself and making a difference. Improving yourself to improve others and creating to make the world better is meaningful.

Everyone has his or her own story around money. Judge your own bank account and not someone else's. If money were the motivating factor, I could have easily stayed in my corporate job and done less for a six-figure income. Money used wisely is a defense. It takes money to build organizations and buildings that help others. There is no reason to be jealous of anyone. You, too, can work as hard to acquire that which you desire.

CULMINATION OF LIFE

> *"Do more than belong: participate. Do more than care:*
> *help. Do more than believe: practice. Do more than be*
> *fair: be kind. Do more than forgive: forget. Do more than*
> *dream: work."*
> —William Arthur Ward

You have a story to share. Whether you've had a life of adversity, trauma, or greatness, telling that story will help someone else. You teach what you've learned and share your perspectives. Your story is worthy of sharing because you are good enough, polished enough, and articulate enough. Sharing your story is truly a gift. How you share it is up to you. Your story is important to the person who needs to hear it.

You have many talents and you make a difference with them. Whether you wire houses or teach acting, you are making a difference every day. You are at your best when you are using your talents. Do what you love, shine, and inspire others. This is your legacy. You master your art and leave it for generations to come. The beauty of sharing your story, time, and talent is you impact others, and this has the ripple effect. By impacting one, you impact many. You give hope.

Friends would tell me to look for a new company; however, there was no point in looking for work elsewhere because I would still feel the same way. I had tenure with this company and had built up company benefits. A new job will provide the same purpose—money to allow me to grow my business— and it actually will take up more of my energy to learn a new job—energy I can better use on my own purposes. It's too much time and energy to switch jobs unless there is a reason attached that will help you fulfill your heart's desires.

You make a difference by developing yourself and then sharing your story and the steps you have taken to get where

you are today. You make a difference by being you. Take
others with you on your journey.

> YOU MAKE A DIFFERENCE
> BY BEING YOU.

The totality of experiences
shapes our lives. The people you meet, the books you read,
the experiences encountered shape you and give you direction.
Muck happens. It is up to you to get out of it and do what
you were meant to do—to bring good cheer and help others
by using your talents. Teaching someone to dance or making
someone laugh can make a huge difference in another's life.
Even if you touch someone's life for a moment in time or a
season in his or her life, it means you are fulfilling your purpose
and helping that person more than you know.

In my life, it feels as though it took me a long time to get
to the point of stepping into my full potential. I reviewed
Maslow's Hierarchy of Needs and compared it to my lifespan.
If your basic needs are not met, you will not make it to the top
of his pyramid of self-actualization. The top of the pyramid
is where you are living out your potential. I am middle-aged
now, so I hope it does not take you as long as it has me to
realize your potential! I am now doing the things I love, and
by doing so, I am helping others realize the greatness within
themselves.

SUMMARY

Starting from my teenage years, I knew I wanted to make a
profound difference. I didn't know exactly what job I wanted,
but I knew I had to do something rather than nothing. Each
experience led to the next, and somehow, it all aligned together
nicely. My work experiences and my education complement
one another. Getting free from the muck was critical to making
my dreams come true.

Knowing myself well enough to understand how I wanted
to shine my light and whom I wanted to serve was the next

step. And the irony—after you have done all the work to "find yourself"—you must let go to become selfless in service to others. Giving to something much greater than ourselves is worth celebrating. Rejoice in these moments; you deserve it.

REFLECTION QUESTIONS

How have you already made a difference in someone's life?

_____

_____

_____

_____

_____

_____

What is one action you will take today to make a difference? Keep it simple; this does not have to be hard.

_____

_____

_____

_____

_____

_____

What would you enjoy doing that would make a profound difference?

_____

_____

_____

_____

_____

_____

What are your next steps to get started?

_____

_____

_____

_____

_____

_____

How can you alter your view of your current job from a daily
chore to an opportunity to prepare to grow your own business?

_____

_____

_____

_____

_____

_____

What skills have you learned at your day job that will aid you
in your new venture?

_____

_____

_____

_____

_____

_____

19

CELEBRATING A LIFE YOU LOVE

*"Imagine doing what you want, when you want, with whom
you want, for as long as you want, without ever having to
answer to anyone . . . that was my dream. My vision. My
ultimate fantasy and it came true."*

—Steve Siebold

What does your ideal life look like? Sometimes, looking back at my life, I should have been in breakdown mode a lot more than I have been, but by the grace of God, that was not the case. It was not until I had a breakdown that I was able to move forward with writing this book. Writing this chapter really got my goat. How could I possibly write about celebrating a life I love when I felt stuck in the muck at a day job that was keeping me from sharing my talents with the world? The dreaded day job was the least of my problems. Let me tell you what my life was like when I began trying to write this chapter.

My adult son, who had turned twenty-six, had been living with me for a few months. Yes, this was the same son who had been stabbed and used meth and heroin. The reason he was living with me was because he was clean. He was attending some prerequisite classes at community college, working full-time, and had been accepted to a prominent school for a degree in Ministry and Leadership. My church asked to photograph him and put him on a billboard advertising its church campaign, "I love my church." His life had made a 360-degree turn. I was ecstatic over the progress he had made in a matter of weeks. He looked healthy. I had my son back! I saw parts of him I didn't realize were there, and I could see myself in him. We shared many moments together with both of us in tears from laughing so hard.

At the same time, my youngest son decided to go to treatment. Once again, I felt the reason he wanted to go was not necessarily because he wanted to change his life, but rather, he was feeling uncomfortable with his living situation. He also had a glimmer of hope from seeing his brother on the right track, though he remained somewhat skeptical that his brother would remain clean. I was hopeful they could both be clean and sober together. I was hopeful that once my youngest son was able to clear his mind and get some sobriety, he would choose the path of recovery.

The same weekend my younger son left for treatment, the older one decided to return to the streets and to using drugs. One evening, I saw him texting someone, and when I woke up the next morning, he was gone. Time continued to move. A letter of acceptance from the school arrived, as did bank statements, medical bills, and legal mail. All of the people who were my older son's support in his new life reached out to him. But there was nothing I, nor anyone else, could do. He made a conscious decision to go back to using drugs, and he made every excuse possible. His attitude reverted back to that of a person I did not like to be around. My son checked out again, and the addict checked in.

At this time, my youngest son kept calling me from the treatment center in California. He was distraught and asking about his brother. Eventually, I had to respond to a direct question from him. I could not lie. He knew his brother wasn't doing too well. The news of his brother's relapse had a devastating effect on him. After he had been fifteen days at the treatment center, I got the call that the center had booted him out.

In times past, I would have put him on the next plane home. Instead, I decided to put myself on a plane to meet him in California. I wanted to try something different. I purchased a ticket, hurriedly packed, rushed to catch a plane, landed, got a rental car, and figured out where I was going in an unfamiliar area. Approximately six hours later, I found him sitting on the curbside at the 7-Eleven Gas Station in Riverside, California. I knew from the moment he told me that he would go back to treatment that he would.

Over the summer, I had seen a glimpse of my older son's real self when he was clean and I wanted to see my youngest son while he was clean. I knew he was going to go back to the same place he had left. I wanted to cherish whatever little time I could have with my son while he was clean. We had a terrific time going to Universal Studios. He always loved cartoons, so Universal Studios was the perfect place to take him. I was also able to drop in on my mother-in-law and my niece. It was a short trip that may not have seemed to impact my son's life at the time, but I am hopeful it did impact him in more ways than I can know. We built memories, and then after about five days, we headed home.

My husband welcomed us at the airport, and we stopped to grab a bite to eat once we got close to home. As soon as we made it to the local restaurant, my son wanted to leave. He wanted to see his brother. No—let's call BS on that right now. He wanted to go get high. Efforts of persuading him to make the decision to stay clean were only as good as the moment. He ended up coming home with us. He started unpacking, and soon piles of laundry were sprawled out in the TV room.

It wasn't very long, and he, too, left—leaving me with heaps of clothes all over.

When both of my adult sons went back to using drugs, I remember coming home from work and breaking down in tears. I grabbed my phone and called a coach that I had worked with a few years earlier. I don't know what made me call her that day. We hadn't spoken in a very long time, but it was like calling a friend, and we didn't skip a beat. We picked up right where we had left off. In the middle of my crying, she laughed; then I laughed. Great. I'm breaking down and my coach is laughing! But the laughter actually lightened the conversation, and it helped me to articulate better what I was going through. I hired her again.

During one of our sessions, she mentioned the importance of having emotional boundaries. I had not thought of boundaries in this way before because I had created physical boundaries with my sons. I was no longer giving them money. I had quit doing certain enabling behaviors. However, this term "emotional boundaries" intrigued me and stuck with me. I needed to process what it meant for me.

I took three weeks off of work, which is something I had never done for myself in the past. During all the things I had been through, I had never taken time out for me. I knew my head wasn't quite clear, so I would not be able to concentrate at work. After going through ten-plus years of watching drug addiction play out in my children's lives, something was different this time.

During my time off, I went to Half Price Books, a local secondhand bookstore. It isn't always easy to find what you are looking for there; the books are shelved spine-out. But there was one book on a stand facing outward in a bright yellow book jacket. It nearly jumped into my hands and said, "I'm going home with you. You need me!" The word "freedom" was in its title: *Emotional Freedom*. This was exactly what I needed at the time. I've talked about how freedom is one of my core values. So this book by Judith Orloff really caught my attention. It cleared some emotions for me that needed to be diminished to allow for the creation of a life I would love.

Also during this time, I started seeing a counselor, mainly to appease the requirements of my corporate job so I could take off three weeks. But this wonderful woman turned out to be on the same page as me. She actually provided great insight and resources. Her compassion and healing presence proved to be a wonderful sounding board for what I was learning by reading *Emotional Freedom*. It was a great experience to bring in the exercises I did from the book and share them with my counselor.

During the previous three months, I had seen changes for the better in my sons and I felt something was different about "this" time. I thought *they* were going to be different this time. This was it. Something changed. Only it was me—I changed.

> THE BREAKDOWN BROUGHT ME TO A NEW PLACE—A BREAKTHROUGH!

I was no longer going to chase after the people I loved the most. I didn't realize it at the time. The breakdown brought me to a new place—a breakthrough! I am no longer going to wish for this dream or that dream for someone else. My life is more than half over, so I am going to pick up the dreams I left behind.

Who says I'm too old? Who says I'm too fat? Who says I can't? And you know what else? Who cares? I'm going to pursue every goal that is still a burning passion within me. Those things we look back on and say, "Oh, I should've," or "I wish I would've," well, I am! There is no such thing as missing your calling. Where there is breath, there is hope. I am still called, except now is the time. It is God's perfect timing. My heart is in the right place. The *why* behind my *what* changed from being self-aggrandizing to selfless for the betterment of others and the world around me. I am no longer the naïve, reckless, ungodly creature I once demonstrated. I am my ideal self. I am reaching the highest level of self-actualization on Maslow's Hierarchy of Needs. The harvest of my potential is coming to fruition. My life is taking on a greater meaning outside of myself. I am going to impact lives for the better and continue to make a difference in other people's lives.

FREEDOM

As I've mentioned before, freedom is one of my core values, so I strive to see more of it in my life. Steve Siebold's quote at the beginning of this chapter paints a vivid picture of freedom. Once I started working with this value and defined what it meant to me, it started showing up in other areas of my life. At first, it meant financial freedom.

I then started thinking about freedom as meaning I could spend my time any way I wanted. Because of my job, if I didn't want to work on any given day, I was not realistically able to take the day off. I had to answer to someone else if I wanted to take one day off in my own life, and it would cost me a day of vacation or sick leave. I didn't even feel like my days are mine. I have to pay for them. However, as Paul Tsongas said, and as has been repeated many, many times, and I will repeat here, "No man on his deathbed ever said, 'I wish I had spent more time at the office.'"

I believe we are not fulfilling God's purpose for our lives when we stay in jobs we despise. God gave us talents, so we should use them. Talents of music, art, cooking, any dang-blasted thing you want to do that makes you happy. When you do something that makes you happy, you have freedom. I believe you can acquire the skill and knowledge necessary to launch your dream—your purpose in life. Add knowledge, skills, and natural talent together and you really have all you need to get started.

Imagine yourself completely free. Free to spend your money how you want, and free to spend your time how you want.

The key here is that you are *spending*, and we all know that once it is spent, it is gone. That may sound like a "take away" that creates lack—once the time is gone, it is gone; once the money is gone, it is gone; once your life is gone, it is gone. But it also makes you realize how precious is the time we are given. Money comes and goes but you only get one life. There are no guarantees. Take the action now to make your dreams a reality.

What I realize now is that while my son was clean, he didn't get the help he needed for the underlying emotional baggage he carries. Instead, he was going through the motions of what we in society classify as a "normal" life without becoming "normal" inside. Treatment is not enough; as I've said, the road of recovery requires internal work. We need to cleanse ourselves of the muck both externally and internally. Muck-cleaning has proven to be an ongoing process for me. I continue to open the compartments and do internal cleansing from time to time as the need arises. The steps in this book—reflect, recover, redirect, and rejoice—are intertwined and to be used continuously as needed. What would it feel like to you to be emotionally free?

I believe people are living on autopilot and feeling stuck. I know people get stuck in their emotions because I have been there. I believe people are working a "job" because the muck of life has taken over. I believe people are in situations where they feel they are stuck in the muck and cannot get out. I believe people have dreams that were lost.

I believe you have God-given talents, and within those talents lies a place of joy for you. I believe you want to live a life of meaning. I believe you want something more for you and your family. I believe you want to live out your dreams. I believe once you make the decision to step forward, everything will come to you. I believe in your dreams, and I believe in you! I believe if Steve Siebold's fantasy has come true, so can mine, and so can yours!

Let's start putting back into this time equation the things you love doing. The things we did as kids that kept our energy levels up—dancing, bike riding, swimming. You are capturing the time doing the things you love! As for money, even though we spend it, each time we do, we are blessing someone else. I spend my money with intent. There is a purpose behind the causes I support. When the money goes out, it flows back in. I love Dave Ramsey's analogy for this principle. When you have a clenched fist while holding your money, nothing else can come in, but when you open your hand and give freely, your hand is also open to receive.

You can also apply this idea to your eating habits to make your weight loss goals much easier to achieve. When we think of dieting, we think about all the things we cannot have, and that thought makes us feel like we are being deprived. On the flip side, when we look at all of the healthy foods we are now going to be putting into our body (instead of taking out), we now have an abundance of food. Instead of looking at it as a "take away," I am replacing foods that lack sustenance with foods that actually fill me up. Instead of looking at it from the perspective of not being able to have something, I look at it as if I have an additional abundance of food that I am now including in my eating. Gradually replacing less healthy foods with whole foods takes the weight off. This has been a process for me, and I didn't do it *all* at once.

We can make these positive shifts in the ways we think about time, money, and food. Working at replacing your old thought patterns is the first step to long-term success in living the life you love! When I have the freedom to spend my time and money where and when I want, I find more credence in my value of freedom becoming my reality.

Get crystal clear about what you want for your life. What is it you want to learn so you can get to your final place of living life instead of slogging through the muck? Here is a list of steps or goals you can use in your journey. We've discussed them all, so now that you understand them, it's time to implement:

- Discover your values and life purpose
- Resolve internal conflict and self-sabotage
- Free yourself from emotional bondage
- Be confident in being you
- Learn self-discipline and self-control
- Transform your relationships
- Gain freedom and be at choice

THE DESIRES OF YOUR HEART

Where the spirit of the Lord is, there is freedom: "For the law of the Spirit of life in Christ Jesus has made me free from the law of sin and death" (Romans 6:18). When I surrendered my life to God, the desires of my heart started to come into my life. The more I seek Him and follow His ways, the more blessed I am. I want more of Him in my life. I want to hear Him loud and clear. Surrendering means getting rid of my ego and becoming selfless; it means serving others. Surrendering means to me, not my way, but His way. I want my steps to be the steps He would have me take. Then the purpose for my life will come to fruition as something much greater than I can even envision.

I have had my struggles and mistakes. The greatest thing of all is that you do not have to make the mistakes I have! You can learn from my pain. You can live a life of hope, freedom, and happiness. When we focus on God's goodness, goodness comes.

"Delight yourself also in the Lord, and He shall give you the desires of your heart."
—Psalm 37:3

No Regrets

"All you need is love. But a little chocolate now and then doesn't hurt."
—Charles M. Schultz

I love organic dark chocolate. Good organic dark chocolate, and yes, I read the label! Chocolate is God's way of telling me everything is going to be okay. When life gets mucked up, rinse it off and see what's underneath it all. Find the meaning, the lesson, or the silver bullet. Turn your challenge into your cause. Turn your adversity into your strength. When I have been faced with a difficult situation, I have asked myself, "If I were to live a life without regret, what is the action I need to take in this particular situation?" Our minds get clouded with emotion and stress, but when we can pause, clear away the muck in our minds, and ask a simple question, the answer is there.

I regret not taking a cruise with my mom. Little did I know she would be gone a year or so later. My husband and I hesitated to go on the trip because of money. It was this mistake that made me determined to be there for her when it mattered most. I do not regret putting my life on hold for three months to be with her at the end of her life. If you were on your death bed reflecting back on your life, would you regret taking a trip with a loved one? Would you regret not pursuing your dreams?

I was in the muck of life. I worked full-time, served my country, and went to college. All of those experiences and the work helped shape who I am today. Those experiences led me to a day job that allowed me to provide for my children. However, I did not have the freedom to spend an exorbitant amount of time with them. I did not have the financial freedom to take them to Disney World or other vacations. I did not have the time or knowledge of personal care so I could always show up and be the best mom. Life happened. Muck happened.

My mother had a high school photograph of herself that I never saw until I went to take care of her while she was going through chemo and radiation. She looks like a movie star in it. I also learned at that time that she liked to dance. Her sister, my aunt, said my mom was always dancing around. Apparently, they sang a little song they would dance around to while cleaning the house. I never knew this until I was with her during her last months of life. This brings me to a point of grieving. I dance around, too, and I wish we could have danced together. The only thing I can think of is she lost her sense of self as muck happened. I never want to stop dancing. I never want to stop being silly.

I don't want another person to get stuck in the muck of life. It is time for you to pursue every dream you ever imagined. Stop living life vicariously through someone else's dreams. Stop making someone else's dreams come true with your time and money! Stop being a wanna-preneur who says, "I want to do this, and I want to do that, but I am full of excuses and too lazy to take action. It is much easier being a victim. It's much easier blaming everyone else in my life for my not being where I want to be at this moment in time." It's much easier to talk about what you are going to do than actually to do it! I believe getting yourself out of the muck, whether it be an abusive relationship, financial hardship, self-sabotaging behavior, or an internal battle of the mind, is a great starting point for becoming free.

Start getting clear on what your dream is and decide you are going to turn over every opportunity necessary to make it come true. Decide what you are willing to sacrifice in order to make room for what is to come. Decide whom you will seek out for support and guidance. Ask for what you want in prayer, and ask for all of the right people, the right resources, and the right opportunities to come your way.

REJOICE!

Celebrate your milestones with the people who love you. Give praise and glory to God for the grace He has shed upon you throughout your journey. Acknowledge those who have helped you along the way. I certainly did not do everything alone. Grab on to the small differences you are making along the way and celebrate those, too! Acknowledge yourself for the work you have done. There is no greater feeling than to know you have made a difference in someone else's life. I trust I am paving the way for other family members to share their stories. I am demonstrating that dreams can come true for my family, and let it be so for you, too.

If you allow yourself to dream and visualize the things you desire, your chances of achieving them are greater. Taking consistent action is required. I like to dream BIG and with that comes BIG responsibility. Impacting lives is not for the weak. I want to be a good steward of my time and resources. I want to use my money to support causes I believe in and experience humanitarian work. This book is the seed that needs watering in order to grow these wishes. This book is the beginning!

I encourage you to dream BIG. Write out what you want your life to look like in one year. You don't have to figure out how it will happen. Just write it all out in as much detail as possible. Start to dream! May you be blessed with health, prosperity, and living your passion! Live and celebrate a life you love.

SUMMARY

Start dreaming again today! Know that you are better than you think. You can have your heart's desires. Focus on the positive and you will attract positive people into your life. Stop settling and going along with the masses of minions! Step out and be you, and then love yourself for it. Live life as if you will have no regrets. Do what you love; of course, you've heard this before. Do activities that bring a smile to your face. Hang with like-minded people who want the same things as you do. Take time to celebrate you and your journey. Celebrate the small and the big things in life. Be delirious in joy and pay no attention to the crazy people around you. Rejoice! Rejoice! Rejoice!

REFLECTION QUESTIONS

What is most important to you in your life right now?

_____
_____
_____
_____
_____
_____

What is something you want to do but haven't? If you were diagnosed with a terminal illness, would you regret not having fulfilled this dream?

_____
_____
_____
_____
_____
_____

What are your next steps?

_____
_____
_____
_____
_____

"It is not death that a man should fear, but he should fear never beginning to live."
—Marcus Aurelius

FOUR STEPS FOR FREEING YOURSELF FROM THE MUCK

Use these steps any time and repeatedly in your life and you will move forward. You will heal, change, and celebrate.

1) Reflect
2) Recover
3) Redirect
4) Rejoice

A FINAL NOTE
DREAMING IN MOTION

Put your dreams in motion. Your dreams are only imagination until you take action. To move forward, you must change the way you think. Expand your mind. Shift thoughts, perspectives, opinions. Challenge yourself and take on things outside of your comfort zone. Read, read, and read some more. Study things you love. Personal growth comes from experience and education.

Hopefully, after reading this book, you have gotten to know yourself better since that is key to becoming your ideal self. Becoming your ideal self requires introspection. Reflect on the most impactful experiences in your life. Look into the mirror and self-assess areas you want to change. Transformation starts with awareness and then action. You can reach any goal or dream if you are willing to do the work. Become your best self so you can live your biggest dream.

If you truly want to achieve your dreams, you must take

action. Consistent action, no matter how small, is necessary. Persistence is key.

I challenge you to become the unstoppable light in a dark world. Be on fire for the difference you make. Start right *now*. Write down three things you commit to taking action on within twenty-four hours to move forward. What will you do within the next twenty-four hours to shine?

I shared with you what were the impact and consequences of some of my choices. In this book, you learned that by reflecting and learning from your mistakes, you are able to forgive yourself and have compassion for others. You realized you are at choice; you do not *have to* "should" all over yourself. Knowing your values and living in alignment with those values is powerful. You begin to recover yourself and reach wholeness, letting go of the guilt, anger, and labels that others have put on you. Being intentional in redirecting your behavior, you learn to go after what you want. It's time to celebrate life instead of doing what every other unhappy person does. . . . do something different. It's time to live *your* dreams and rejoice!

My mission is clear: To use my gifts of boldness, humor, and leadership to propel you into action so you can make the difference you've desired. Face your muck so it's not repeated with your kids and grandchildren. Then celebrate a life you love and teach future generations how to do the same. Together, we can make a profound difference in our own lives, in those of our grandchildren, and for generations to come.

Thank you for reading this book. Please help me get this information into the hands of someone you know who could use it. Leave a review at online retailers or contact me directly.

Now that you've read the book, what's next for you? Take action, and *expect* results. When you believe in yourself and your dreams, expect it to happen, take the necessary action, it will happen. Your dreams will come true!

RECOMMENDED READING

Acuff, Jon. *Quitter.* Brentwood, TN: Lampo Press, 2011.

Blume, Judy. *Are You There God? It's Me, Margaret.* Scarsdale, NY: Bradbury Press, 1970.

Carson, Richard. *Taming Your Gremlin: A Guide to Enjoying Yourself.* New York, NY: William Morrow, 2008.

Emerald, David. *The Power of TED*: The Empowerment Dynamic.* Bainbridge Island, WA: Polaris, 2009.

Ferriss, Timothy. *The 4-Hour Workweek, Expanded Updated Ed.* New York, NY: Harmony, 2009.

Huch, Larry. *Free at Last.* New Kensington, PA: Whitaker House, 2004.

Goleman, Daniel. *Emotional Intelligence.* New York, NY: Bantam Dell, 2005.

Greenleaf, Robert. *Servant Leadership: A Journey into the Nature of Legitimate Power & Greatness, 25th Anniversary Ed.* 1977. Mahwah, NJ: Paulist Press, 2002.

Medina, John. *Brain Rules: 12 Principles for Surviving and Thriving at Work, Home, and School.* 2nd ed. Seattle, WA: Pear Press, 2014.

Millburn, Joshua Fields. *A Day in the Life of a Minimalist.* Missoula, MN: Asymmetrical Press, 2012.

Orloff, Judith. *Emotional Freedom: Liberate Yourself from Negative Emotions and Transform Your Life.* New York: Harmony, 2009.

Ramsey, Dave. *The Total Money Makeover: Classic Edition: A Proven Plan for Financial Fitness.* Nashville, TN: Thomas Nelson, 2013.

Siegel, Daniel J. *Mindsight: The New Science of Personal Transformation.* New York, NY: Bantam Books, 2009.

Snow, Patrick. *Creating Your Own Destiny: How to Get Exactly What You Want Out of Life and Work.* Hoboken, NJ: John Wiley & Sons, 2010.

Ziglar, Zig. *Zig Ziglar's Little Book of Big Quotes.* n.p.: Zig Ziglar, 1990.

ABOUT THE AUTHOR

In *Muck Off*, Carol L. Lopez shares her experience of how abandonment affected her self-esteem, which resulted in decisions and behaviors that led to a painful life. Never feeling like she was good enough or valued, she spent her life on a journey of recovery. She decided it was time to change the way she felt, harvest her potential, and pursue her lost dreams. Today, she is passionate about helping people get free from the muck and mire of dysfunction in order to live with true purpose and meaning. She believes you can be happier and live a fulfilled life by freeing yourself from emotional pain and pursuing your dreams. Carol has found healing through her creativity in acting, writing, coaching, and speaking.

Originally from Markham, Illinois, a south suburb of Chicago, Carol joined the US Navy when she was nineteen and retired from the US Naval Reserves. Carol worked primarily in the field of Human Resources in both the public and corporate sectors. She has a graduate degree in Organizational Leadership from Gonzaga University. Her undergraduate degree in General Studies from Columbia College includes a concentration in psychology and a minor in criminal justice. Carol completed transformational coach training through an International Coach Federation (ICF) accredited school. After leaving her corporate career, she started her coaching business.

Carol has transformed her life and loves helping others who are serious about getting to where they want to be. She has been through the muck and has found that when you are willing and courageous enough to "Reflect, Recover, and Redirect, you will Rejoice!"

Carol has been married for over fourteen years. All of her children are adults. She and her husband are enjoying their empty nest and currently reside in the Seattle area, although she loves sunshine and palm trees!

BOOK CAROL LYNN LOPEZ
TO SPEAK

Carol Lopez has spoken in front of hundreds of people. In her presentations, she shares relevant stories that are customized to the topic of your choosing. Carol brings hope, courage, and inspiration to her audiences. She has a sense of humor grounded in a no-nonsense attitude. Topics she desires to speak about include personal care, leadership, self-development, recovery, and transformation.

Don't delay in getting free from the muck to start living *your* dreams. Contact Carol to hire her to speak or to work with her as your coach. Hire her to coach your employees and leadership team.

For a complimentary, thirty-minute consultation to find out how Carol can help you, contact her at:

coachcarollynn@gmail.com
or
www.MuckOffBook.com

CPSIA information can be obtained
at www.ICGtesting.com
Printed in the USA
FSHW011021111119
63972FS